Mini Escapades around the British Isles

D1449822

What they're saying about

BONNEVILLE GO OR BUST
On the Roads Less Travelled

Zoë Cano's first solo expedition across America

"A thrill on two wheels! An up-close-and-personal tour of Americana!" *MetroWest Boston Daily*

"Best bits are the colourful, vivid local encounters!" *Wanderlust* Travel Magazine

"An unputdownable tale!" *South East Biker* Magazine

"*Bonneville Go or Bust* is proof that it can be done, and that adventure is more about your mind and opening it up. Give it a read and be inspired." *Traverse* Magazine, Australia

"Zoë's actually combined her love of travelling & motorcycling with her inherent ability of stringing words together to capture the imagination of her readers." *Bike Rider* Magazine, New Zealand

"A 6,000 mile odyssey!" *Asphalt and Dirt*, USA

"A totally inspiring and motivational story" *Back Street Heroes*

"Her written descriptions are vivid, detailed and engaging." *Overland Magazine*

"She passed her test and headed off for the USA. Straight away. Like you do!" *MSL* Magazine

"Her research is deep, the descriptions strong and her connections with other people are open and friendly. Each of these meetings is like a pearl on a necklace!" *Adventure Bike Rider*

Road Dog Publications was formed in 2010 as an imprint dedicated to publishing the best in books on motorcycling and adventure travel. Visit us at www.roaddogpub.com.

ISBN 978-1-890623-78-4
Library of Congress Control Number: 2020946155

Cover design by Olwen Fowler

An Imprint of Lost Classics Book Company
This book also available in eBook format at online booksellers. ISBN 978-1-890623-79-1

Mini Escapades around the British Isles

by

Zoë Cano

Publisher
Lake Wales, Florida

"I travel not to go anywhere, but to go. I travel for travel's sake.

The great affair is to move;

to feel the needs and hitches of our life more nearly;

to come down off this feather-bed of civilization,

and find the globe granite underfoot and strewn with cutting flints."

Robert Louis Stevenson

ABOUT THE AUTHOR

Zoë Cano, whose first name means "Life," is an adventurous spirit.

Born in the English border town of Hereford in the 1960s, she very quickly moved to live and work in Paris for ten years before moving to New York and, finally, Boston, with extended periods in Brazil and Asia for the international events business.

Zoë started rowing competitively and then took the challenge to skiff the entire length of the Thames, from its source in the centre of England to Greenwich, London.

Among her many exploits, she has crossed the Peruvian Andes on horseback, motorcycled numerous times solo around different parts of the world, and still travels extensively.

Zoë lives in London and is also the author of the highly successful and recommended travel books *Bonneville Go or Bust*, *Southern Escapades*, *Chilli, Skulls & Tequila*, and *Hellbent for Paradise*.

For more information on Zoë Cano, her books and travels, please visit www.zoecano.com.

CONTENTS

PROLOGUE

JOURNEYS CLOSER TO HOME

"Beauty and adventure often lie no further than our own backyard."

Over the years, I've been fortunate enough to spend a large majority of my life living in different countries and travelling to far-flung, distant lands. In some respects, I feel I was lucky—at the time when I travelled—to visit these places as they were then: The People's Republic of China in the 1980s, when people in the streets just curiously wanted to reach out and touch you to see if you were for real and well before motorcars were introduced, with everyone cycling everywhere and still wearing Chairman Mao's military grey uniforms or the obligatory white T-shirt and grey shorts; Paris, before it had its first fast-food Burger King on the Champs Elysées; the relatively unknown Cuba, when Castro still ruled and spoke every day for hours on the country's only television channel; Thailand, when Bangkok's closest beach of Pattaya still only had one hotel; the never ending untamed Brazilian Amazon Rainforest that hadn't yet been massively and tragically deforested by illegal loggers; and the tropical paradises such as the empty Phi Phi Islands in the Andaman Sea with their pristine white sands, which were still relatively unknown and difficult to access.

Since then, over just the past few decades, the world has become a much smaller place; and rapid, cheaper travel to the other side of the world has become almost normal and, for most, no longer an impossible luxury. But times are changing, and people are becoming ever more aware of their carbon footprint and the way popular tourist destinations, from climbing Everest to visiting Venice, are becoming destroyed by the masses from their original unspoilt beauty. People are becoming more mindful and even considering "staycations," instead of planning to travel.

Over the years, I've also managed to criss-cross closer to home throughout our beautiful British Isles and found I'd done quite a number of interesting and diverse trips on various forms of transport. I felt it would be a great idea to compile some of them into one book. This compilation of short stories, encapsulates the beautiful, diverse, and pleasantly surprising places that sometimes don't get first priority when we decide to travel or take a holiday.

But I've long been a convert and amassed an even greater love of the British Isles, realizing just how lucky I am to be living in such a wonderful and eclectic place. We have all four seasons, so we experience the ever changing landscapes at different times of the year. There are no language barriers, and once out of the large cities, there are soon more than enough places to go and explore: England's beautiful green countryside, lakes, seaside towns, and history; Scotland's spectacular scenery with ancient castles, windswept beaches, and historic landmarks lurking around every corner; the wild, unspoilt ruggedness and genuine hospitality of Ireland; the natural quiet beauty of Wales with its national parks, hidden valleys, and beautiful coastlines. For such a small place, we really are spoilt for choice.

As I near completion of this book, it's Saint Patrick's Day, 17 March 2020, and nothing will ever be quite the same as we live through these unknown and uncertain times. The coronavirus (COVID-19) pandemic is spreading uncontrollably across the world, and we're fighting an invisible battle to desperately find a cure. Europe's borders are closing, and America is not allowing anyone to enter. Towns and cities everywhere are in shut-down, and people are being advised, or forced in certain countries, to self-isolate and stay at home. My friend George, living in the City of Light, told me today, "Paris is in total lockdown, and we're needing an official piece of paper just to leave our homes! The joyful streets of Paris are empty, feeling a bit like a ghost town." Another friend, Véronique, from Paris sends me a homemade face mask, one of many she's making for her neighbours.

With less movement, there's less pollution. With no boats in the Venice Canals, the waters are clearing, and for the first time in living memory, fish can be seen swimming in them! The choking smog in cities is disappearing, with people on the Pakistan borders witnessing for the very first time in their lives the snow-clad Himalayas hundreds of miles away.

Just a week later on 23 March, a monumental statement is announced to the nation by our Prime Minister, Boris Johnson, that "we're in it for the long haul" and that Britain will go into indefinite lock-down. No one is to leave their homes, except to access food and medicine, do essential work, and do an hour's exercise while strictly maintaining the new phenomena of social distancing. Strict rationing has been enforced, with supermarkets saying no one can bulk buy and that priority must be given to the elderly, the most vulnerable, and essential workers like the doctors, nurses, care-workers, and supermarket staff, who have now become our heroes. All schools, pubs, restaurants, and social venues, including most parks and beaches, are now closed. No mass gatherings are allowed with any unnecessary social interaction. More than one million stranded British people all over the world are desperately scrambling to get back home. More than three billion people worldwide are in lock-down.

The following early spring morning, with the apple blossoms shyly appearing and taking my allowed once-daily walk, the streets are empty, besides one other person with a face mask coming towards me. We shyly nod and smile, our faces hidden, but he's quickly crossed the street to avoid even closer contact. It's eerily quiet, like the world has gone to sleep. With no traffic, the louder and more highly defined sounds of chirping birds are now heard, from the blackbirds, thrushes, sparrows, blue tit, robin, wren, goldfinch, London's green parrots, and cooing wood pigeon, and these birds are constantly sighted throughout my garden and surrounding neighbourhoods. Simpler but essential things without a price tag are becoming highly prized: a solitary butterfly landing in my garden, watching the newts play in the pond, speaking with friends and family, staying healthy, and endeavouring to smile every day while counting my blessings.

We can only pray to whatever or whomever we believe in that we are all kept safe and healthy in these never before seen times and that, very soon, a cure will be found and we will all be given back our cherished freedom to go out, explore, and experience our world close or far from home.

"I am speaking to you at what I know is an increasingly challenging time. A time of disruption in the life of our country: a disruption that has brought grief to some, financial difficulties to many, and enormous changes to the daily lives of us all . . .

We should take comfort that while we may have more still to endure, better days will return: we will be with our friends again; we will be with our families again; we will meet again."

Her Majesty Queen Elizabeth II—5 April 2020

PART ONE

Good Old Blighty!

So, let's start from the beginning. Throughout my life, I've held a stronger than normal affinity to water and everything that exists in, on, and around it. Water in all its guises, from warm tropical aquamarine seas, crashing oceans, peaceful lakes, strong flowing or slow meandering rivers to small trickling mountain streams have always felt like essential life blood to me.

Hypnotic. Peaceful. Energetic. The same medium that enhances and stimulates all five senses. Quietly sitting on a beach watching the animated dancing of waves with each sequence never quite the same as the last or witnessing river tides rise and fall brings inspiration and positivity to me that life abounds around us on this beautiful, fragile place we call Earth.

From my earliest memories growing up, water had a role to play to make me a stronger, more inquisitive, and maybe a bolder, less shy person. Before I knew it, before I could probably even walk, my hero, my father, had taken me with my unbearably tight swimming cap and red rubber ring to the local pool at the Bishops Meadow in Hereford. Over the years, all I could remember about that hot, humid place was the acrid smell of chlorine, the fear of catching a verruca while walking through the shallow water to the pool, and trying to avoid and navigate around the used plasters and tangled hair bobbing on the surface. But I loved that floating sensation and, somehow with the feel of weightlessness, it gave me a sense of freedom that would lead me later on in school to swim competitively.

Sadly, my mother couldn't swim—like most children from her generation—as she just hadn't had that opportunity while growing up during the Second World War in the 1930s' bomb torn industrial city of Stoke-on-Trent in the Staffordshire Potteries. But I believe it maybe goes deeper, as she had been cruelly pushed into a park pond when little by a thoughtless boy and, unable to keep afloat, became frightened of water for the rest of her life.

The first time I saw the sea and felt sand trickling through my little toes and curious fingers was back in the '60s on a simple family holiday in Blackpool, overlooking that cold dark expanse of the North Sea. I couldn't have been more than four years old, but my memories are still vivid of holding onto that donkey for dear life as I was led along the beach. And just a few years later, my younger sister, Lisa, and I were treated to our first international holiday and much warmer climes in the still relatively unexplored and unexploited Torremolinos on the Costa del Sol in Spain. To say my father was in his element was an understatement, and with his fluent Spanish, we were treated and introduced to all the local specialities, including paella and flamenco dancing. Unbelievably, he even cleverly coerced a group of roaming Gitanos to hand over their giant prancing Andalusian horses and let my little sister and I ride off on our own. I'll always remember that sound of the wild, out-of-control clattering, trotting hooves racing up and down the rough tarmacked palm-lined road—with our dangling legs too short to properly fit into the stirrups, and all beside that hot, clear blue Mediterranean Sea.

Many summers were spent deep in the English countryside with my Matthews cousins swinging and jumping from branches into the water and swimming in the quiet River Cam near Grantchester and Cambridge. Still dripping wet, we'd walk across the green river meadows to a little tea house for strawberries and cream or to eat huge picnics on the riverbanks during those hot, hazy days. At the time, as children, it felt like the place was there only for us. School holidays were also spent exploring idyllic Loch Lomond in Scotland, where Lisa and I would excitedly sleep on our own in a small moored up boat, hearing the calming ripples banging the hull while the adults slept close by on the little island. The Famous Five had nothing on us!

And the river brought food to the table in the most unexpected ways. One evening back in the '70s, a knock was heard at the kitchen back door of my parents' Somerville Hotel, where we lived while my mother ran the place, responsible for cooking and sourcing the food. Her talent in the kitchen, having been one of the first British Gas demonstrators back in the 1950s to teach the burgeoning middle-class housewife on how to cook for a family and cater for the ever-growing social occasions, was second to none. She opened the door to find two very young boys shyly looking up at her while holding something almost as big as them! They'd just caught a massive, wild pink salmon from the River Wye and immediately could only think of one person in Hereford who'd discreetly take it off their hands. My mother didn't question its origins, as she'd seen her mother do the same when bartering for food on the black market during the Second World War, and quickly exchanged for it by putting a generous number of coins into their little hands. That night we and the Somerville guests were treated like royalty to the most delicious "illegal" meal.

The River Wye in Herefordshire was one of my favourite places while growing up. Just outside Hereford, near the Carrots Pub, I'd sit peacefully in the long, wild grass on the steep river bank to watch salmon leaping out, a bevy of swans elegantly glide past, the flash of blue as the kingfisher dived into the river to catch its prey, rainbow translucent dragonflies, sand martins swooping over its surface to feed on insects then disappearing into muddy river bank nest burrows, and cattle contentedly swishing their tails while quietly drinking its water on the pebbly riverside shoreline.

Even when I left home at the age of nineteen in the early '80s to end up living in Paris for almost a decade, I'd spend hours walking the banks of the Seine and sitting outside its riverside cafés simply watching life and the watercraft pass by. Hot sunny days would be spent in the Parisian outdoor lidos, including the famous Art Deco Piscine Molitor in the posh sixteenth arrondissement, where its three levels of white painted changing cabins made it resemble a large ship and where, some even say, was the birthplace of the bikini!

Water also provides memories of sheer, unadulterated passion, love, and eroticism. Lost in wonder on small uninhabited Thai islands that at the time had barely been explored by the outside world yet, swimming in its most pristine clear sea, floating in an abandoned private swimming pool high in the hills overlooking Los Angeles, or stranded on sand bars in the Caribbean—and all shared with a loved one. Feeling that warm water and the other person's tingling body sensually and slowly caress your entire body has no comparison—pure heaven on earth.

Returning to England in the '90s after so many years away, I turned to the river again and started to row competitively and to make life-long friends, including my best friend, Lulu. Life at Teddington's Walbrook Rowing Club also introduced me to skiffing, the traditional hand built, clinker-built wooden craft of a design originally used by ferrymen on the River Thames and other waterways in England for nearly two hundred years.

This resulted in a handful of us crazies navigating with several skiffs the entire 180 miles of the Thames, from its source in Gloucestershire to Greenwich in central London. Shortly after that escapade, Lulu and I both decided it sensible to embark on another crazy plan: to take our Competent Crew course. So, it was decided to undertake a one-week sailing course on the Solent during what must have been one of the most freezing cold Februarys in history. But with those exams and practical experience under our belts, doors mysteriously opened to other opportunities. A chance encounter just a few months later occured at work with a freelancer named Scott, who just happened to be an avid sailor and boat owner, who introduced himself and invited me to take up the opportunity to crew his yacht, which I enthusiastically grabbed with both hands!

Over the years, water has been intrinsic in so many ways to help me find peace and inner calm. When my father finally passed away, the first thing my mother, sister, and I did was to walk along the River Wye in Belmont and spread his ashes. I was devastated, needing to find solace, and once again with the desire to escape to peaceful waters. So, just a month later, I found myself in Jordan's Red Sea, with the excuse of taking my scuba diving PADI training and exams. Over the years, this resulted in diving and exploring the seas across the world, such as in Cuba in the quiet Caribbean and the extreme opposite in the Maldives, which are surrounded by the challenging strong currents of the Indian Ocean. And this is where I began to see the dangers of these vast waters and how easily anything could be swept away.

The jaw-dropping and vast expanses of water around the world were again seen when working in Brazil. Waking up with nature before dawn in the Amazon, watching the massive sky turn gradually scarlet red, hearing the echoing sounds of macaws and howler monkeys in the forest while silently paddling down the Amazon River with the sun slowly rising from the horizon's eastern edge will be one of the memories I will cherish forever. Kayaking through the wild, steep, glacier-carved and ocean-flooded giant Fiordland of New Zealand and straining my neck to look up at the unimaginable steep sides of the snow-capped Southern Alps while floating at water-level and peering down into the bottomless depths brought the magnitude of nature's forces just that little bit closer to home.

Throughout my life, with everything I'd experienced on and under the water, including naturally a number of new and unexpected challenges, I was pleased to say that nothing whatsoever dangerous or even life-threatening had ever happened to me, except for maybe the time our eight-crewed rowing boat uncontrollably crashed and ripped apart into Kingston-upon-Thames Bridge during faster than normal winter currents, and which resulted in us appearing on the front page of the local paper. But all that was to change when I met and went sailing with Scott! Nothing would prepare me for what I was about to encounter out at sea on his boat.

THE SOLAR ECLIPSE ADVENTURE

SETTING OFF AND SAILING
ACROSS THE CHANNEL

1999 is going to be a year to remember in good Old Blighty! While everyone and their mother are beginning to get excited and starting to plan on how they are going to uniquely celebrate the new millennium at the end of the year, I'm thrown an unexpected invitation later that summer that I just can't refuse. I'm to celebrate something totally different but just as important.

Looking up from my desk in the corporate wing of Reed Exhibitions in Richmond-upon-Thames, I see a stocky silver-haired sixty-year-oldish guy approach with that familiar smiling, cheeky face. His short height also gives him away as a lucky sailor, as he could probably just about stand under a boat's boom without too much bending down. It's Scott, whom I'd got to know while chatting at the water fountain and where we found out we both had one thing in common, sailing!

That loud, almost guttural, Scottish voice shouts over to me, "Hey, Zoë, Good morning! It's my last day contracting here today, but you really should, like I've already said, come down to Southend-on-Sea for some sailing where I keep *Artemis*. And I know it's late notice, but I'm also planning a bit of an adventure in August and need an extra crew member and, well, thought of you."

My eyes light up, but I'm hesitant, as I really haven't had any sailing experience besides the five day Competent Crew course earlier in the year and don't really know if I'd be a strong enough pair of hands for whatever he had in mind.

Scott continues in his strong namesake's accent with an air of rushed excitement, "Och aye, it's not going to be just any old trip. It's going to be us sailing during the total eclipse of the sun, which will be on the eleventh of August. The last total solar eclipse visible from the UK mainland and surrounding area was a long time ago on 29 June 1927, and the next one after this year isn't until 2090! So, I guess you could say a once in a lifetime experience! We'd sail from my marina in Southend with two other crew member buddies, and the general plan will be to get in the central path of the total eclipse, which I think will be somewhere across the Channel, off the coast in Northern France and close to Fecamp. So, the trip shouldn't last more than a handful of days. And then we'd all become a member of "The Full Eclipse" Club. What do you think?"

I'm almost licking my lips with hidden excitement but cautiously reply, "Gosh! I wasn't expecting such an offer. Thank you! In theory I'd love to, and I've still got some annual holiday left over. But I just hope I'm going to be skilled and helpful enough for you. You need to know I've had very little experience."

Scott claps his hands like a little kid and chuckles flippantly but then adds in a somewhat sobering and reassuring way,

"Aye, great stuff. Don't worry. Sharon is a highly skilled and proficient sailor with years of hoisting sails under her belt, and her husband, Ozzey, is just as good at making bacon butties and tea! I swear I won't even wear a kilt but only serious sailors' waterproofs. We'll have a hell of a time. As a frugal, tight-fisted Scot, I might even buck the trend and splurge out and pop some champagne when we witness the sun's total eclipse!"

One month later on a busy Friday summer's evening coming out of London with all the sweaty commuters, I jump onto a train to Southend-on-Sea in deepest Essex, which was the appointed meeting place. It was just before seven when the train pulled into the station, and although a little early, I soon hear the impatient honk of a car's horn, with Scott waving his arms from the driver's seat of an old Volvo Estate crammed full of stuff in the back.

We drive through the empty country lanes and marshlands to the Marina, where we quietly park the car among moored up boats and unload our bags onto a trolley. I politely follow Scott down and along the pontoon until we get to the skipper's recent acquisition, a Hunter Horizon thirty-footer, called *Artemis*. Its shining white hull and tall mast look pretty impressive to me, and it appears a hell of a lot bigger and more comfortable than the boat I'd crewed on in the Solent earlier in the year.

Soon after we've wheeled the empty trolley back to the parking lot, the rest of the crew, Sharon—a frizzy haired and red-lipsticked smiling lady—and Ozzey—a tall and robust geezer—arrive with waving arms and park alongside the Volvo. Seeing their excited and happy smiles, I just know we're going to hit it off as we get their kit and food supplies stowed onboard. Immediately, Ozzey steps into action, and true to his word, produces a gourmet salad from the little galley kitchen and serves it up on plastic plates. Small bottles of wine pulled out of a cupboard, and courtesy of British Airways, are dutifully consumed by all.

It's then that Scott's face becomes slightly sterner than the initial merriment. "Alright, I guess we've got to get this over and done with. I'm going to give you all a tour of the boat and show you where the life-saving equipment can be found—life jackets under those seats on deck, which we should wear at most times, the harnesses, which we should ideally strap on when the sea's rough or we're moving up and down the boat, flares in that cupboard, radio and horn in the cabin."

All three of us seriously nod in unison, and little do I realize at the time just how important all this equipment would be later on in the trip. That evening as darkness falls, Scott knowingly points out the special navigation lights around the marina and harbour area. We even see one or two intrepid sailing boats setting off down the river with their red and green lights facing forward telling us where they are and in which direction they are going. Passing us at the marina, their white light at the rear confirms that they are, indeed, sailing away from us.

After some consultation with the charts, forecast, and tide tables, it's agreed that the best time to start would be 06.00 hours the next day on Saturday morning, when the tide would be with us at the all-important "Gull Stream"—wherever that was! The wind we're told was to be coming from the north-east so wouldn't be very helpful until we'd travelled some fifteen miles to clear the River Crouch, where we were currently moored.

The accommodation was sorted. Sharon and Ozzey would get the triangular cabin at the front known as the forepeak but which looked mighty cramped for a woman and her very generously sized man; the skipper had his master cabin at the back that was already piled high with his crumpled clothes; and I was to use one of the settees in the main cabin. I stowed my bag under the settee and that evening was rocked to a peaceful sleep in the quiet marina.

I awoke to the shuffling of feet in my cabin. Scott was already on the move and sighing with impatience. "Morning. We've overslept. It's already 6.00 hours so we need to leave fairly shortly. Hey Sharon! Wake up! We're already late, and we need to get moving!"

On that early Saturday morning on the 7th August I was told my first job was to learn how to release the mooring lines from the boat without ending up in the water myself. Then, when the boat was "underway," to untie the fenders from the sides and stow them properly in the locker on deck. This was all done quickly as we motored our way out and said our goodbyes to the marina. I was quite surprised to see that we were the only boat leaving at that time.

Scott, like a true Captain, was at the helm as he shouted out orders to us: "So we're bound for Dover with ETA of about 17.00 hours. Sharon can you come on up and take over, as I need to get onto the radio."

And with that, he leaps down into the cabin, calling up the Thames Coastguard on the VHF radio and confirming our plans so they could log us on their Traffic Computer System. Early that morning we motored past the sleepy looking town of Burnham, with dozens of boats moored out on the river itself, and on into more open waters. After about half an hour clearing that lot, we put the sails up for the first time and start to use the wind to drive us forward. So far, we had passed some green buoys that marked the left-hand side of our "road" and one or two red buoys that marked the right-hand side. It was then I see my first cardinal, a black and yellow buoy that apparently marked some danger—or something like that.

By now Ozzey, who always seemed to be hungry, is busying himself with preparing breakfast for us all. He'd promised us a major fry up with eggs, bacon, sausages, tomatoes, and a ton of tea. But as time wears on, and our stomachs rumble even more, the wind starts picking up strength, causing the boat to uncomfortably lean over a lot, as I also start to desperately hang onto the side. And with the rocking movements, Ozzey is having more and more difficulty handling the hot fat below! With a worried look, Scott just about manages to peer down into the cabin to see what the hell's going on. "Hey, listen up! It's now far too dangerous for the cooking to continue. I'm afraid I'm going to have to request you stop the process. Please turn the gas off now!"

It's then I hear lots of spillages and noise below—eggs are lost down the sink while the pots and pans seem to be flying everywhere. Poor defeated Ozzey can't finish preparing his special breakfast and is ordered by the captain to immediately come up top to join in the normal duties of just sailing the boat. For an hour or two we struggle against the wind to get the boat clear of the river. The wind eventually settles down to some form of consistency, letting us stabilise the situation and collect the remnants of the food that had been cooked so we are able to have at least some sort of breakfast. It is only a lot later after the trip that I am to learn that cooking should only be done when the boat is docked or anchored, and this includes grilling bacon!

Possibly due to the extended periods of instability on board or lack of sustenance, the worst conceivable thing at that stage in the journey happens to me. I suddenly feel uncontrollably weak and nauseous. It is the beginning of a serious bout of horrible sea sickness. I'm certainly not feeling well, with already a weak stomach, and can't even manage much of Ozzey's special breakfast. The boat is now leaving sight of land and turning south-west to start crossing all twenty-six miles of the wide Thames estuary. My queasy stomach is sloshing back and forth and my mouth is tasting acidic. And it is there in the middle of this massive river that I lean over and "feed the fish." No matter where I look, no matter where I sit, no matter what I do, I continue to feel dreadful, with not an ounce of energy. Every so often I stick my head out over the back and uncontrollably perform, once again, only leaving that evil rancid taste and smell in my mouth and an increasingly raw, sore throat. Each time I think I have nothing more to give, my stomach is again painfully wrenched, squeezed, and twisted to expel every last drop. My sickly pale face is hanging so much over the bow now that the salty water painfully splashes back onto it. I have no physical strength to move away, but just lie there.

The rest of the crew try to console me with promises of betterment. I can barely imagine anything else while I sit sprawled out, lifeless on the deck. With all my energy gone, it feels like I'm just fighting to stay alive. I just want to go home and be in my nice warm bed. But there is no way to escape. That, in itself, is frightening. Time stands still as time apparently does when one is in pain. It is then that the wind drops to almost nothing. They put the engine on, saying that this would help me feel better. I can assure you that it does not. With my face overboard and now breathing in the engine's horrible diesel fumes it makes me feel even more sickly and weak.

Eventually, after hours of agony, I begin to feel extremely cold and am shivering, and decide to go below and lie down. Sharon helps me slowly down, lays me on the bed, and spreads a blanket over me. The awkward motion of the boat continues relentlessly and my feeling of utter dismay and why I'd even decided to embark on such a ridiculous journey, totally out of my comfort zone, continues. It is only a lot later in the trip that Sharon tells me that they were very concerned about my state of health but were unable to help very much.

It is towards the end of the afternoon, at around 16.00 hours, that we divert to Ramsgate to get some fuel, after mooring up in their marina. Hallelujah! It is now much quieter and calmer and miraculously I quickly begin to recover from my stupor.

The seaside town of Ramsgate, in the "Garden of England" county of Kent, is a place well worth investigating as I begin to remember what it is like to walk upright as we stumble ashore and finally put our feet onto steady land. We head to the imposing yacht club with its splendid posh viewpoint overlooking the harbour, shoreline beaches, and the general hustle and bustle of the waterfront below. Here, I slowly sip a glass of water, still trying to recover my balance but now feeling desperately hungry, as there is no question that my stomach had been totally emptied! The Thai restaurant next to the club looks and teasingly smells wonderful with its exotic spices wafting our way, but it is already fully booked, so we make do with the Chinese food around the corner. With our lack of sustenance and overspent energy used up relentlessly during the day, the others set about eating like pigs at a trough, consuming tons of chow mein and sweet and sour, while I'm more than happy to opt for simpler fare. And all the time clutching my chopsticks, I'm trying to recover that elusive equilibrium! That night, totally exhausted but warmly wrapped up in my sleeping bag, I thankfully doze off and sleep a lot better than I could ever have imagined. Good sleep to charge the batteries is paramount as it is going to be another early start.

In Ramsgate Marina the tides dictate when you should leave. The noisy whistle of the steaming kettle in my cabin wakes me up like an alarm clock, and through the port hole, I can see it's still dark. Scott is, as usual, shuffling around, rustling paper, and inspecting unknown bits and pieces.

"Morning Zoë. Knock on their door, will you, and shout for the guys to show their faces. It's just gone 5.30, and today the tide will go with us from 04.00 till about 09.00 and then start to go against us from about 11.00 till 16.00. So, we kind of need to leave latest around 06.00. Get yourself sorted, put all your stuff away, and see me up on the deck."

On that early Sunday morning I am appointed to rope duty as we slowly motor out of the marina, and this time, much to the captain's glee, we manage to leave on time at 06.00 sharp. The general plan is to get to Brighton in East Sussex and call in at Dover en-route. The blowing wind is still coming down from the north-east at a force of 4, gusting 5[1][see end of chapter]. Happily, the boat sails well, and I feel a million times better from the previous day's hell. That might be because part of my recovery medicine, administered by the rest of the crew, is to steer the boat. This means concentrating carefully on the direction we are headed at all times. Although my tummy feels just a bit queasy, I manage amazingly to concentrate hard on the task in hand and successfully retain the contents from last night's meal!

On the south-eastern tip of England, the pretty seaside town of Ramsgate, with its historic Royal Harbour, soon falls into the distance as we pass the twin twelfth century Reculver Towers of Deal. The view of the headland sometimes bob up and appears, making us feel we are getting closer, but then it will suddenly and mischievously disappear, making us feel like we are still far out at sea. Although it is only about twelve or fourteen miles away, the two or three hours that we take to get to Dover, on the heel of Kent, passes pretty slowly, with nothing major to report. And it's true that I'm a little nervous at the outset for fear of becoming sick again, but I'm persuaded to sit on the highest point of the boat and to use the tiller extension. Eventually, we arrive at the headland, with views of the disused windmill and the old lighthouse both standing on the top of the cliffs.

And then it happens. The skies suddenly darken and unexpectedly open up, soaking us all, despite wearing our various rain resistant clothes. And even with my waterproof jacket and trousers, the rain still somehow gets in and creates a sodden, cold layer over my skin.

As we reach St Margaret's Bay, which we reckon was only about four miles away from Dover, the tide unwantingly starts to turn against us. Our progress is almost brought to a complete standstill, with the sails flapping wildly around us. It is strange to see that we are still going through the water at the same speed, but our progress against the land is almost nil. From the weather forecast we're tuned into, the station is telling us that the wind is about to shift round to the south-west. This is pretty bad news for us, as we are wanting to go in a generally south-western direction.

Heated debates with the captain ensue on what we should do. It is obvious that we are making little or no progress against the strong tide, and as well as being cold and wet, it is unanimously decided that we should quickly get into Dover.

By now the cross-Channel ferries are visible. Those lurking within Dover Harbour look gigantically enormous. Those that appear suddenly from over the horizon move quickly and appear like they are coming down onto little us in a most threatening way. How would we get out of their way? Scott quickly jumps down below, moving the VHF radio to the correct channel, and hears Dover Harbour Control's cool, calm, and collected voice. It is controlling every vessel within the area like someone calmly conducting his orchestra to achieve a sweet, smooth, and organised melody.

Suddenly, Sharon rushes and jumps down into the cabin. "Hey Scott give me that radio. You know what I like!"

With that, she calls the harbour master with her sweet female tone of voice, "*Artemis* is requesting that we come in on the eastern entrance. Thank you."

Almost immediately, she receives our standby orders, followed by the usual "ma'am" that she likes so much and which makes us all let out naughty giggles. Eventually, we are instructed to proceed through the entrance, while we make good speed with the engine on. The vastness of Dover Harbour is eye-watering and as large as many a holiday bay. As we push forward at our steady pace, we witness and look up at one of the enormous passenger and car ferries that had come in and was smoothly turning around on a sixpence to its parking place next to the harbour wall. This whole commercial harbour is enormous, but are greeted by friendly instructions from the Harbour Control about how we should proceed. We simply pootle across this vast bay and down into the protective and enclosed sanctuary of the marina that provides a welcome rest from the driving rain and all that bumping around. Miraculously, I've survived it all and am now starting to feel much better about this sailing business!

With the engine turned off and the boat securely tied up, a serious "Decision Making Council" is formed with Scott and his ever loyal crew. If the wind is now coming from the west, then should we not go south? Apparently, that would be a good direction for sailing in these sort of unreliable conditions. If our ultimate goal was to see the eclipse, then this could be done from here by going west or south towards France. And besides that, which excites me the most, is an opportunity to return to French soil with all that tempting fine food. The votes are cast and south it is.

Old sea-worn Skipper Scott is jubilant and, rubbing his hands, announces, "Great stuff mates! Now all we need do is get the appropriate flags. We'll need a red ensign for the boat itself and a French tricolour to be used and hoisted as a courtesy flag!"

After a sandwich lunch in the cabin, we all head through the streets of Dover to see if there is some sort of a flag shop open on this quiet Sunday afternoon. Nothing remotely like it, but while walking back, Lady Luck was smiling as we caught sight of a yacht chandlers open on the seafront. And it does, indeed, have the two flags Scott is adamant in getting for the onward journey.

I smile and turn to face everyone, "I'm just going to get a newspaper, and I'll get some essential goodies like anchovies, tuna, eggs, and olives for a Salade Nicoise, which I'll make for us all tonight. We are, after all, going to France tomorrow!"

Sharon smiles, "Merci Mademoiselle. Ozzey and I are going to grab a beer at a pub, and then we'll catch you later back on the boat."

Later that evening, after a scrumptious meal and one too many glasses of wine, Scott looks down carefully and seriously at the maps, "OK guys, tomorrow we're crossing the channel, and this is going to be a critical exercise for us all. We need to get it right, with extra caution and consideration for the tides and wind. Sharon, come on over and agree with me that this is the route we need to take."

With their heads peering down at the nautical map and knowing I can't really assist that much with the technical strategy, I politely excuse myself and jump off the boat with a towel over my shoulder to head over to the marina's shower block. The showering experience is pretty decent, with exceptionally hot water. But on returning and tapping the numbers on the entry gate back to the boats, the security gate just doesn't want to open and let me in. After what you could call a bit of struggling with impatiently pressing and re-pressing the buttons, with mobile phones still not commonly used to shout for help, with the help of a passing sailor, I finally get back to the rest of the crew. Unbelievably, they're still looking at the nautical chart, with Scott quizzically scratching his head. The atmosphere feels just a teeny bit tense, with no doubt, the impending trepidation of what we were going to do tomorrow, and so without much to do, everyone politely decides to retire for an early night's sleep.

On the fourth day, Monday 9th August, the wind is still blowing from the south-west at about 3 or 4. Fortunately, we don't need such an early start, and Ozzey makes a cracker of a breakfast around 08.00 AM before we leave the marina about thirty minutes later. We're totally out of the giant harbour by 09.00 AM, with Sharon receiving her customary "ma'am" on the radio as we clear the western entrance. It is, after seeing them so close up at sea level, that I'm grateful that the ferries, sea cats, and hovercraft aren't competing to leave at the same time as us! The waters would have churned up, and we would be crazily zig-zagging to avoid them!

For that first hour or so we have no other choice but to head straight into the wind, with the noisy fume-belching engine powering us on. The waves are noisily splashing over the top of the bow, with the wind blowing any excess cold spray directly towards and onto us. I push my scarf further up and over my chin and lips just to keep a tiny bit more protected from the freezing water. It's about at that point that the always diligent Sharon goes below for an extra wooly hat, to only then discover that seawater is somehow ominously seeping into their cabin at the front.

She screams up to Scott, "Shit! The hatch isn't properly shut, and our bedding's getting soaked!"

You could say we have no other choice but to stop and sort matters out, which involves us emptying the compartment of all the bedding, pillows, clothes, and anything else they'd brought, hanging some of the stuff up to dry inside the main cabin, and then battening down the hatches as tightly as possible. It is clear we now had to proceed a hell of a lot more slowly to prevent the battering volume of water coming over the bows and leaking in again. And this makes our progress even slower.

It's then I start to see out in the far distance large ships going down the channel that the others knowingly point out to me, and all I can think to say back is, "How interesting!" After some time of painfully slow motoring, we finally decide to pull up the sails, as apparently this will be better for the splashing effects that we're experiencing at the bows. Progress is slow and laborious, but at least we've all managed to get up on the upper part of the boat again, and *Artemis* skips through the water in a happier mode than it had done with the engine.

Scott pulls down his sea-sodden yellow hood and seriously looks out in front while steering the boat, beckons me over, and shouts against the howling wind, "We're coming to the point where we're going to cross the shipping lanes. It's extremely important that we cross at a specific angle so that the ships can see us and know that we're crossing."

At first, it seems just like any other stretch of water, and because we had turned our direction in the wind, we were now skipping along quite nicely. Then they, or let me reword that, the experienced ones start all of a sudden getting highly excited about which of these gigantic ships were going to pass in front of us and which ones would not. Will we get there first? Or will we be like a sitting duck in the line of fire? Discussions start getting fairly heated, especially when we discover we don't even have a hand-bearing compass to calculate these precise and essential seafaring measurements. As one enormous ship approaches us in dangerously close proximity, it's decided, at what feels like the last minute, to stop and wait to bob up and down in this vast channel until the unstoppable giant has sailed past us. The ship is getting so dangerously close that I'm almost convincing myself that it could actually end up ramming into us.

To say I'm scared is a slight understatement, so I give the polite excuse in order to disappear from this unfolding nightmare, explaining to one and all that it's time for me to "inspect the heads," or toilets in layman's lingo. And in that tiny little head, without daring to look out of the equally tiny port hole, I pray with clenched shaking hands that my crew know what they're doing and gambling our lives on. When I finally emerge back up on deck, things feel slightly calmer. We had indeed, sensibly stopped and waited to let the enormous ship continue on its unstoppable way northwards towards Scandinavia. This successfully done, we set off again in the given direction towards France, ready to face the next obstacle or challenge.

After a while, we arrive at the "Half Way Point" in the channel. I suppose it can be compared a bit like a traffic roundabout in the middle of the ocean, but that the channel edges have no markings at all and very few buoys. So, all these quick manoeuvres, stopping and starting, are happening in front of me in open water, and I just have to accept the old skipper's word on it all. On our "traffic island" the sea is noticeably rougher than it had been, due to the shallow depths and tidal flows in and over this patch of sea. But once we're clear, we then start crossing the next channel, and this time constantly looking out for ships coming in the opposite direction from the west. This time, they're a little more difficult to spot, because we're sitting with our backs to the giant vessels. However, to tell the truth, although there are one or two ships heading in our general direction, thankfully there are no scary close encounters like we'd had earlier on.

We cover and cross this lane in about an hour and then turn due south to pass Cap Gris Nez, the headland between Calais and Boulogne, and the French headland closest to England. This pretty much represents the shortest distance across the channel from Dover of eighteen-point-two nautical miles, or twenty-one land miles.

Once again, we find ourselves fighting a losing battle against the tide, becoming slightly rougher off the headland. And it's taking quite a while just to cover the fourteen miles down to Boulogne-sur-Mer. In the end, we give up, with no other choice but to turn the engine on and motor the last few miles. Once again, *Artemis* and the crew are confronted by a large outer harbour with its giant protective walls of the largest fishing port in France. Inside, on the calm waters, we motor in to find a smaller section in the far corner where the marina and its yachts are located.

I reckon we've arrived at the perfect time, as we're offered a parking spot next to the thick stone wall, which is also conveniently right next to all the facilities. It's only later on in the day that other yachts and gin palaces arrive. Mayhem is starting with the number of boats arriving, and most have no other option but to unusually raft up against one another, as there's now just no more room in the marina. By the end of the day, we unbelievably have about ten other boats rafted up and tied onto us. Tomorrow, we'll be physically unable to move away until all the others have sailed off! Maybe there are masses of boats here because of the eclipse happening close by in just two days' time and the vessels are racing to get to the right location. But it's also peak holiday time, all the schools have closed for the long summer holidays, and so, sailing families are naturally out in force.

The first place you normally become familiar with in a marina are the toilet and shower facilities, but unfortunately, here they're less than perfect compared to the delightfully pristine ones we'd been spoilt with in England. But walking into the old fishing town of Boulogne, soaking up the continental atmosphere, hearing French being spoken once again, drinking coffee on the terraces, and buying fresh seafood from the outdoor marketplace more than makes up for the lack of perfect facilities in the marina. That evening, we leave *Artemis* and wander into the historic part of Boulogne town and decadently dine on oysters and a fine white muscadet. All is well with the world, and I now feel that I'm getting the hang of this sailing lark. But little do I know what is yet to come!

[1] *The numbers are in the Beaufort Scale, in which conditions are refered to by "Force" numbers from 0 through 12, shown below. Wind speeds in knots.*

Force 0, Winds 0-1, Calm

Force 1, Winds 2-3, Light Air

Force 2, Winds 4-6, Light Breeze

Force 3, Winds 7-10, Gentle Breeze

Force 4, Winds 11-16, Moderate Breeze

Force 5, Winds 17-21, Fresh Breeze

Force 6, Winds 22-27, Strong Breeze

Force 7, Winds 28-33, Near Gale

Force 8, Winds 34-40, Gale

Force 9, Winds 41-47, Severe Gale

Force 10, Winds 48-55, Storm

Force 11, Winds 56-63, Violent Storm

Force 12, Winds 64-71, Hurricane

LOOKING AT DEATH IN THE EYE
OF THE STORM

I lazily yawn, open my eyes, and pull the cabin's curtain back from the port hole to be greeted by sunny blue skies, but also noticing that we were still trapped in by eight or nine other boats. Knowing there's not much we can do to escape, I roll over and try to snooze off again.

Scott appears from his cabin wearing just his baggy greying Y-fronts and immediately sets about leaning over the stove, unknowingly putting his bum in my face! Heating the kettle up, he shouts through the main cabin to the closed door in front, where the others are still probably asleep, "Sharon! Ozzey! I'm making drinks. We've got to talk and plan about what we need to do. This is the day before the eclipse, and we need to get to the right spot today! Stop doing what you're doing and come on out!"

With all four of us still in our nightwear, looking slightly dishevelled, hugging mugs of coffee, and sitting on the two long seats in the main cabin with the table between us, Scott is the first to talk. "Now listen up. We're about forty-five miles away from the eclipse zone, and we have two options. Either we set off in the afternoon with the south-going tide, or we wait until early tomorrow morning and scoot off in the dark to get there by about 10.00 AM."

Even I think the second option is a bit optimistic on timing, but I say nothing and just quietly listen to what the others are thinking and have to say. Sharon chirps up, "There're a lot of boats around wanting to probably do the same thing. Let's try and get there early, so there's less hassle to find marina space and to give us time for any unforeseen stuff and also avoid sailing in the dark. I vote for this afternoon."

Everyone else happily nods in unison to opt for the afternoon run south. But not before Scott adds with a slight concern on his face, "That's good, and the wind is predicted to be 4 or 5, still helping from the north, but there are serious rumours here in the marina that it might just pick up later on in the day. To be truthful, I'm also concerned about getting into Valery-sur-Somme without a suitably detailed chart, so I'll need to go and get one from the chandler's, but that shop doesn't open until 2.15 this afternoon, which leaves things a bit tight."

So, after tidying everything away and lounging about smelling the waft of Gitanes, Scott goes out on his mission and successfully purchases the new chart. With the boats that had been tied up to us long gone, we set off just a little after 2.30 in the afternoon and immediately hoist the sails outside the harbour. Just half an hour later, we turn our tail to the wind, and the boat wonderfully flies off at five or six knots. Progress is excellent in that warm afternoon sun, layers are peeled off, suntan cream plastered on, and I'm really enjoying, for one of the first times, some smooth, hassle-free, fast sailing. We watch across the waters as the various hazy coastal towns appear in front of us then disappear just as quickly behind us. This is the life!

Earlier that day while lounging in the marina, we'd met a couple of friendly French guys doing the same route as ourselves in a yacht called *Tameras* They were planning to go to Le Treport and had been one of the lucky boats able to free themselves and set off well before midday. Scott curiously calls them up on the VHF radio to determine where they currently are and how things are progressing along that part of the coastline. They confirm they are, in fact, already forty-five miles ahead of us, and apparently, the weather is still great. Scott smiles, sighs, and happily claps his hands hearing this piece of good news about the weather and the fine sailing conditions.

As the day wears on our progress is still excellent, and we're all in good spirits, with Ozzey even able to boil the kettle and make us a brew. All my sea sickness has totally disappeared, and I feel like a new person since we'd left England. Somewhere and at some stage, out at sea the wind mysteriously picks up. But as we're running with the waves, we hardly notice that they, too, have dramatically picked up their speed and size. We are effectively now uncontrollably water skiing down them. The boat is now occasionally also slewed from one side to the other as we get to the bottom of each enormous wave. Even Sharon at this point declares she doesn't like the current sailing conditions, with the violent and uncontrollable turning and sliding actions of the boat.

Around mid-afternoon, we sight two distant yachts sailing north-bound and directly into the wind. They bounce from one wave to the next, with spray continuously flying up and over the crew. On a few occasions we notice the whole boat appears to dangerously come out of the water, heading and jumping skywards, and then splashing down with a tremendous crash and the whole vessel stopping dead in the water. I can only think what a terrible journey these sailors must be having as we carry on in relatively flat conditions, with only the occasional wave overtaking us.

By early evening, around 18.00 hours, we should be making our way up the River Somme's mouth entrance to find protected mooring. Scott is standing, looking out from the helm, "I hate to say this, but things are becoming very dangerous, because the waves are now just too high, and we just wouldn't have enough deep water to sail up the river as planned. We'll be bounced along the ground at the foot of each wave, damaging my new boat. I've got to urgently think what we can do. Sharon we've got to quickly come up with an alternative solution to get us and this boat somewhere safe!"

Here we are amongst waves that had become eight feet or more in height, and we simply aren't able to get up the estuary to the planned safety of Saint-Valery-sur-Somme, which was annoyingly just a short distance away. As Scott and Sharon had expressed, our options are now somewhat limited. We could press on to the next harbour at Le Treport which was some fifteen miles away, or sail even further down the coast to Dieppe, which was twenty-four miles away but maybe a better bet, as it was open at all stages of the tide.

The sky by now was becoming ominously overcast and darkness would be with us very soon. Very quickly, the decision is to get to Le Treport, as it is the nearest. But it is only there and then that I learn from Scott that, without a nautical map of this new area, we don't possess any detailed knowledge of Le Treport harbour, the safe entrance line to be used, and any dangers which could be lying in wait within the area. Would this place even have room for us?

By now with a sense of urgency, Scott has, without expression, zipped up his waterproofs, with us all mirroring his actions ready for the unexpected.

He screams out across the wind, "Let's give *Tameras* a call to find out the information. Sharon, go give them a call on VHS channel 16, the emergency and calling channel."

Without hesitation, Sharon nods and dutifully goes below deck and desperately tries to make contact. There's simply no response. She persists again and again and again. And there's still no response. We're on our own. The little boat is now sailing on both sails at a slightly different angle to the wind. By now, we're racing along at eight or more knots, with the waves quickly getting higher and higher that Scott is reckoning are, incredibly, more than ten feet. They're angrily throwing us around like a truculent baby throwing its toys out of the pram.

We can only hang onto the boat for grim life, looking at each other in terror, as it tosses and plunges into the waves' dark black ravines! With life belts securely fastened and tied onto the boat's rails, the sky above us continues to just get darker and darker. Everything now seems to be taking on another surreal dimension and is becoming ever more serious. Dear Ozzey peers down at the chart for any inkling of shoreline and reassuringly reckons that we should already be able to see a lighthouse on the chalk hills, approximately five miles in front of us. There's nothing remotely to be seen within eyesight, other than some distant town lights beginning to glimmer through the grey and eerie light.

By now, we're desperately and continuously checking the coastline to find anything that might just look like Le Treport's harbour lights. Then the lighthouse is seen and has begun its nightly flashing routine, more or less where we expect it to be from the chart reading. This is at least a partial relief that we're now beginning to find the crucial landmarks. And after a while, a flashing green light also begins to appear and blink in the watery distance. Maybe that was the harbour entrance! But stupidly we can't be sure, as we'd never intended to go this so far south with no detailed maps of the Seine-Maritime area in Normandy.

Progress in the almost complete darkness has become much slower, as the tide has turned and is now flowing against us. This is definitely not what we wanted. So, the turbulent last few miles seem to take forever in this vast cauldron of waves and the sea's confusion under our little boat. At this moment in time, I genuinely feel that the sea is ready to consume and engulf us at any moment. We have no control.

Slowly and steadily the green light gets just that bit closer, and its counterpart, a red light, also begins to be sighted by our bedraggled and brave skipper. All this time he's been at the helm battling for dear life to just keep the boat on course and the sails filled as much as possible. The wind is howling and shrieking, and our voices are just getting lost out to sea. We press steadily onward until we're finally only about half a mile away but feeling like an unsurmountable thousand miles!

Scott screams out against the wind, "It's time now we take the sails down. But we've got a major problem. The jib, front sail, has got entangled with its roller reefing mechanism, so we won't be able to put it away. Someone has to quickly go up front to release it before we get into the harbour! I need someone's help to volunteer. I can't go myself, as it's essential I keep a steady and strong hand on the tiller."

Without hesitating, brave Sharon puts her hand up. "I'll do it. We can't put the other two in danger."

With this assignment agreed, Sharon makes sure her harness is securely clipped onto the boat and shuffles her way forward to the offending mechanism. In almost pitch darkness it's difficult to see much. The relentless bashing sounds coming from the boat pointing directly into the ferocious wind are almost deafening. What can be seen of the waves, they seem scarily as high as mountains, and the poor boat is pointing directly into each one as they arrive and cruelly batter her.

Sharon manages to wedge herself into the front railing (pulpit) and struggles helplessly to get the jammed unit to work. During this time, the waves continue to arrive and crash over the front of the boat, thundering down each side of the deck to flood over us. And Sharon, up front, disappears completely from our gaze at the arrival of each large wave. As the boat re-emerges from the watery grave, so does Sharon, who is still wedged in and fighting furiously to release the jammed mechanism. Two, no three times she disappears, and then after what seems like an eternity, she re-appears much to everyone's relief. My heart is palpitating and drumming against my chest. At this moment, I truly feel we're beginning to lose total control, and maybe our lives. Memories start flooding back of how fragile life can be. There had been two other occasions in my life when I thought death was near. The first time, when I'd been diagnosed with encephalitis of the brain when living in America, and secondly, when I crashed into a tree and fell into unconsciousness from the back of a race horse, both leaving memory and physical lifetime scars.

And then a massive rogue wave comes over and floods the boat, drenching Sharon so completely that her life jacket is triggered into uncontrolled action. The expanded life jacket breaks out of its red container, taking on a life of its own, rather like a blow-up doll. It mercilessly forms a firm ring around Sharon's neck and chest. At that point, her head is forced to look up, as the life jacket is designed to do, ensuring that she can breathe if immersed in the water. But this now means that Sharon can no longer look down and see what she is supposed to be doing. She's forced to abandon the foresail and return to the relative safety of the cockpit.

It's at this point in the chaos that the engine's throttle is accidentally knocked to full speed ahead, making the effects of the oncoming thrashing waves even more "exciting"! It feels like we're tumbling around in a washing machine. Working from the cockpit, while looking up all the time, Sharon takes down the main sail and hangs onto the flogging remnant for all she's worth. There's now just screams and shouting going on to just try and be heard above the cacophony of the storm's winds and waves.

So, to put it simply, we've gone from reasonable control in tough conditions to absolute chaos in the space of less than half an hour. With the engine now adjusted at moderate speed but the sails flapping about in total disarray, we motor steadily towards the beckoning harbour lights.

"Will we be alright?" I remember asking. To which all the crew give absolute assurances that we were in no real danger!

I must confess that this doesn't seem to be the case at all, as far as I was concerned. And all of this chaos is not yet over!

We approach the old harbour's entrance between the green and red lights, only to discover a solid stone wall looming up directly in front of us. Only at the last moment do we realize that the long entrance is actually to our left, or "port," side. We turn into the entrance channel with only a few feet to spare, with the boat bouncing heavily up and down as we motor through. Le Treport harbour, another fishing port on the French coast, is in fact, fairly large but currently only dimly lit by the town's lights that surround it. Despite all this, it offers very little protection and respite from the rough seas in and around us. Worryingly, the waves in this confined and potentially dangerous area appear to be just about as bad as they had been out at sea. It feels possibly worse now, because we can actually see the state of the sea beyond, as well as the crashing waves all around us in this small, confined area.

Being careful to avoid the other boats that are moored in the enclosed waters, we stooge around while sorting out the sails and generally making the boat finally ready for entry to the safety of the marina.

Scott shouts out to me, "Zoë! As you speak French, go and take the VHF radio and find out what we need to do to get into this bloody marina!" After some quick instructions from Sharon on how to use the radio, I speak with the harbour master, only to discover that it's impossible, as the marina is now completely full, and we're simply instructed to stay in the stormy harbour and ultimately "dry out" as the tide falls later on in the night.

Once again, Scott looks dismayed, "This is more bad news. The tide won't drop for at least another five hours, to leave the boat's hull standing on the bottom, which means we're going to have to keep on our toes, and we won't get any sleep. Let's at least try and get the anchor down."

And that we do, but the anchor just won't hold in this undulating cauldron of water that in any other circumstance should have just been a calm pond. We strongly believe that all this is due to the abnormal effects of the imminent eclipse the next day, which was changing everything. At this same wild moment another boat comes in under full sail. It's a massive racing trimaran with a main hull and two smaller outrigger hulls attached to the main hull with lateral beams. On hearing our plight through the radio and seeing our waving arms, we use both boats' engines to perform a macabre dance in this gloomy light. Perhaps we could tie up to the harbour wall? The trimaran makes a sterling effort at this and appears to be successful.

So, we also decide to follow suit and make ready with lines fore and aft and as many fenders as we can possibly find to protect our dear *Artemis* from the harbour wall and the waves crashing up against it. We manoeuvre to within just two feet of the wall and desperately have no other choice but to throw our lines to the crowds of curious bystanders, who are by now enjoying the spectacle we're providing! However, as we get perilously close, within a foot or so of the wall, it becomes clear that the protection of the fenders put in place would soon get thrown out of the way as the boat rides up and down like a bucking bronco. Just guessing, I reckon we're going up about eight feet with each wave. And this is the best protected side of the harbour, so the other areas are going to be considerably worse.

Our poor skipper can see his boat is being scraped and badly damaged on the stone wall and desperately shouts out, "Quick! We need to abandon this and get away! Get away! Zoë, scream at those people on the jetty to let go of the bloody ropes immediately!"

I shout out desperately, "Laissez! Laissez!" but some of the bystanders, who are still stoically holding our lines, don't seem to realize that we've given up on this idea. And so, all four of us scream the same words, "Laissez! Laissez!" and use crazy hand signs to persuade them to throw the ropes back on board. But for whatever reason, whether they think they're trying to help save us, they continue to desperately hold on, despite our crazy and out of control screams. There is now significant danger that the boat will be dragged and crash into the harbour wall if they stubbornly continue pulling in on the lines. In the nick of time, with us all still shouting, they're persuaded to let go, and *Artemis* finally turns for the safer waters in the middle of the harbour, missing the jagged wall with only a few inches to spare.

And with that, we continue to pootle around while a number of fishing vessels appear from out of the locked area that leads to the marina. We're now at full high tide, and the waves at sea are now strong enough to, incredibly, pound over the outer harbour wall spraying some twenty or thirty feet into the air like a large blue whale expelling moist air through its blow hole. Indeed, within the harbour, the waves in some places are also smashing onto the harbour wall and sending spray some ten or so feet up and over onto the surrounding road. And in the middle of this little lot we merrily and tirelessly bounce around. During this time, from the depths of darkness, an enormous commercial fishing ship slowly and serenely arrives. It's accompanied by tugs and pilot boats, and we're hearing on the radio that the skipper is seriously concerned that his unusually rough wash, combined with the waves, might even overturn some of the little boats in the harbour.

By now, in what seems like a lifetime, we had spent more than two hours in the harbour area ceaselessly motoring around and had more or less accepted our plight. We were wet, cold, and shivering. The tiredness and exhaustion on all our faces was plain for anyone to see. Then without the slightest warning, the radio comes to life and calls out to us that we can finally enter the marina! We don't need to hear that a second time as we motor speedily into the open lock. It gently closes behind us, adjusting the water's height and letting us into the inner sanctum. We pass all the fishing vessels until we reach the safety of the little marina. It's quite impossible to describe the difference between the tranquillity of the smooth, flat water on which we're now floating compared to the harsh environment we'd just left. We discover that two chaps who managed the marina had returned to work, due to the sea's chaos, and had opened the marina section especially for us orphans of the storm!

Parked up in this quiet marina, we all let out a sigh of relief and immediately open up the good old British Airways mini wine bottles in celebration that we are all still alive. Later on, dried out and feeling a lot better from a comforting warm dinner, we can do nothing else but fall into a deep sleep as a result of the pure nervous exhaustion we'd endured all day long.

THE DAY AND BEYOND OF THE ECLIPSE

We are already six days into our incredible sailing trip, and Wednesday 11th August 1999 has arrived. This is the day of the eclipse, and we are now in the zone of complete cover when the moon will totally hide the sun just after eleven in the morning. The nightmare weather conditions from the previous night have weirdly disappeared into oblivion. The weather is miraculously looking good with, thankfully, much calmer waters. General consensus is given that we all definitely want to witness the spectacle out at sea, rather than in the confines of the harbour area.

Soon after devouring delicious bacon butties and a strong brew, we excitedly take our turn with the other boats to go through the lock and are released back out to sea. The day is relatively clear, with only a patchy covering of clouds, which is what we wanted and needed, and the wind has dropped to almost nothing. Our skipper uses the engine to clear the harbour, and as we chug along and move away at a steady three or four knots, we're witnessing hundreds or maybe thousands of spectators starting to assemble out on the cliffs and hillsides around Le Treport to also witness this bizarre spectacle up in the skies.

As time passes, we take out our one set of special protective glasses, which I think we'd been given free from the *Daily Mail* newspaper before we'd left the UK, and excitedly take turns viewing the sun to see if any changes are happening. Slowly, the moon finally begins to cover the sun. As time moves on there's little change to the intensity of the light until about five or ten minutes before the total event.

Scott points out past the boat and out to sea "That's strange. Look! Those sea birds are flying straight for the land. They don't look happy, and it looks like they know something strange is going to happen!"

I nod. "And what's also unusual is it's now getting definitely a lot colder."

At this point the noisy engine is cut off, and we're left silently bobbing on the surface of the calm water. The intensity of the light is now also noticeably changing. Various hues of blue out on the horizon that I had never before experienced, are verging into a deep dramatic purple as the moment arrives. The white of the boat takes on a waxy appearance, and our shadows become fuzzy against this whiteness. It continues to become colder, and the sky turns dark, not the black of full night but certainly very dark and enough to notice some stars where only moments earlier there had been none. The six or seven boats' lights floating around us become quite clear, as I suppose ours do for them.

The sun itself can now be seen as a corona with knobs of fiery light sticking out from the covering disc of the moon. On the horizon the town lights unexpectedly and automatically come on, and multitudes of cheering, clapping people that had come to view the spectacle along the cliffs all take flash souvenir photographs, giving a firework quality to the proceedings.

To the south of us in the Dieppe area, the sky maintains its dark covering as far as the eye can see. To the north of us, maybe some twenty miles away, it is obvious that the area was less dark. After our allotted two minutes or so of complete shadow or darkness, the light re-appears. Its arrival appears with a dramatic and sudden burst, almost as though someone had turned on a light switch, and within a matter of just a few seconds, we are back to virtually normal daytime light intensity. Yet, when we curiously use the special glasses to check the progress of the eclipse, it's clear that only the smallest amount of direct sunlight is actually flooding back onto us. With a sense of mesmerisation and being totally spellbound, we continue watching the sun and moon parting company, taking turns with the one set of glasses until perhaps as much as twenty-five per cent of the sunlight has returned. Most things have returned to normal, except for the temperature, which is taking a lot longer.

The moment of celebration has now arrived. The champagne is popped open, with its cork flying out to sea, and the oysters brought out from the cool box. The sky has been completely clear throughout the whole event, and the sea, now relatively calm, means there's no danger of crashing into other boats.

Putting the empty bottle of bubbly in the cabin, Scott's smiling face reappears. "Well, I guess we'll need to set off back to Boulogne on the engine, as there's absolutely no wind that can help us. Amazing how things can change in just twenty-four hours!"

Sharon is intently looking at the map. "After some calculations, it's clear that we won't get to Boulogne until well after dark, even with the engine pushing us along at five or so knots."

By now, most boats had left and there are just one or two other boats in the vicinity. It looks like they too are pushing northwards at the same speed as we are, so we keep company with them at a mile or so apart for quite some time before our relative paths separate. As we press on, so does nightfall. The shadows develop, and the lights of the towns on the coast appear. The steady flashing of the navigation buoys become our only landmarks. The steady green and red lights of other ships moving across the horizon are like a slow and macabre dance.

Gradually, in almost pitch black, the strong green flashing light of Boulogne-sur-Mer harbour appears in our field of vision. Just half an hour later, we're gently motoring past the familiar giant walls into the harbour entrance and making our way across the large bay towards the three green lights that mark access to the marina. This time we gratefully hear there is indeed room and that we're welcome to motor in. Unsurprisingly, with all that had happened that day, the marina is full beyond normal capacity and bursting at the seams, so we have no other choice but to raft up next to another boat who is also rafted up to another boat closer to the marina's quayside. Politely stepping over the bows of at least five of our neighbour's boats and onto the pontoon, our rumbling stomachs lead us down the cobbled streets to find a place which will satisfy our hunger and quench our thirst after the day's adventure.

Nestled comfortably in my warm sleeping bag and, following a deep sleep in the main cabin, it's unbelievably very, very early the next morning when I'm suddenly awoken by hearing someone loudly banging on our boat. It's barely light. Someone on the inside of our raft unsurprisingly wants to get off so we, as well as all the other boats tied together, have no other choice but to move and let them out. It's like a pantomime show of weary-eyed sailors trying to be helpful, and after we've all untied ourselves from each other, unbelievably, the original party of sailors change their mind and decide to stay!

Without too much exaggeration, there are at least one or two more-than-angry sailors from the general comments I overhear. "Merde" is an understatement! However, the outcome more than compensates for the inconvenience. In the move from the flotilla, we find a spare "proper" parking slot that has become free, and we quickly grab it. Although it's only about 5.30 AM, none of us really feel like going back to bed. As it's my last day with the crew before jumping on the ferry to get back to work, I happily volunteer to search out a boulangerie for some freshly baked, warm croissants, and over some fresh coffee, we chat about how uniquely adventurous our entire trip has been.

The adrenalin-fuelled excitement of the last few days has not yet ebbed away, and that feeling of having shared something special with friends who could relate to the same feeling was priceless. Time quickly moves on to mid-morning, when my ferry back to Dover is due to depart. I simply walk round to the other part of the harbour with Scott and buy my one-way ticket back. The others will sail back across the channel tomorrow to Ramsgate and then finally, on Saturday, cross the mouth of the Thames and then head up the River Crouch to Scott's home port in Southend.

It is unquestionably a successful and safe end to a wonderful adventure. Later, reading the papers back on the train to London and hearing snippets from friends who'd stayed on terra firma, I realized just how lucky we'd been to see the whole eclipse. Most of Britain had been clouded over, and few, if any, had actually seen the whole spectacle with a cloudless sky as we had. Even Scott's friend, who had sailed his yacht down to Cornwall, had to contend with a dull and overcast day and saw nothing of the actual eclipse. We also later heard that even the people at Le Treport and on the French coastal headlands, less than ten miles away from us, had to contend with some cloud cover during those critical two or three minutes.

How fortunate we were to arrive and survive the storms and to have ringside seats at one of the world's greatest spectacles of the twentieth century.

Less than two years later and on the same boat, sailing along the English South Coast with Scott and best friend Lulu, I get phone reception and learn of my father's unexpected passing. I need to immediately get back home. And with that, motoring as closely as possible to the shore, I jump off the boat and leave the skipper and the remaining competent crew member in the shallow waters. With my duffel bag flung over my shoulder, and salty tears running down my face, I wade through the muddy sand to shore, waving goodbye to *Artemis* for the very last time.

PART TWO

CYMRU

Wales is a very special place to me. Some of my most cherished and memorable moments of innocent childhood days and growing up as a young teenager were spent in Wales.

Cwmfforest was a typical old, white stone, working farmhouse lost in the valleys of the Black Mountains (Y Mynyddoedd Duon) within the Brecon Beacons National Park and close to the market town of Talgarth, Powys. Back in the 1960s, my mother's friends, Mike and Maria Turner, unknowingly became pioneers of the true adventure travel experience. Mike knew all about exploration, as he'd worked on scientific missions on ships to Antarctica in the 1950s.

People started to come and stay in this remote unknown place and ride their Welsh Mountain ponies for hours or even days across those bleak, wild hills inhabited only by the thick fleeced grazing sheep, roaming untamed native ponies, and red kites swooping and hovering overhead. So wild was this place that the SAS, from their secret HQ in Hereford, would ultimately use the farm's bunk house as a base for their extreme military training in these mountains.

Our parents gifted us with early independence. At the respective ages of just six and seven, my sister Lisa and I were dropped off one cold winter's weekend into the warm hospitable arms and care of Maria, who ultimately became like a second mother during the school holidays we'd spend at Cwmforrest. Although less than thirty miles from Hereford and just across the border in Wales, the place felt like another world. This was our first unaccompanied holiday, and time away from home and things would never be quite the same again.

Everything was new to the senses on that Welsh farm. Black and white sheepdogs and their puppies came running up to us wagging their tails and excitedly licking our faces; giant white hissing geese flapped their wings racing scarily after us to grab our ankles; hens pecked at the ground with warm eggs in the outbuildings always ready to be collected; hunting ferrets were gently taken out of their boxes by John, the handyman and horseman, while we tentatively held onto them, making sure to keep away from their tiny needle sharp teeth; mile high stacks of sweet smelling hay were climbed up and jumped into within the warm sanctuary of the barn; the constant trickling noise of the stream coming down from the mountains and along the farmhouse; farmers' sharp deafening whistles instructing dogs herding sheep down the lanes; the distant neighing of ponies in the green hillside fields; the smell of newly cleaned saddles and bridles with leather wax; the crackling wood in the fireplace; clothes hanging to dry over the Aga cooker; the sensation of walking barefoot over strange fur pelts thrown over the floor providing basic warmth; muddy boots left outside the kitchen door; cats and kittens pawing at the door to be let in; robust homemade stews; egg and bacon breakfasts with hearty crusts of bread setting us up for the day; old stone hot water bottles to take away the chill from our freezing cold single bed we shared, where the only other warmth came from hugging each other and feeling the tepid warmth of the chimney wall behind the bed from the downstairs fireplace; sheepskins as extra blankets; carefully carrying candlestick holders to light our way up those old wooden stairs that reflected strange ghostly shadows against those white stone walls; the yet unknown sounds of the night with the howling winds and intermittent hoots and screeches of the night owls; mice scurrying under the floorboards; and then finally, the welcoming rising sun for another new day of new experiences.

And then it was us excitedly riding through those wild Black Mountains with John closely by our sides. That sharp, cold air blowing through us gave us space to see new things.

I relished those moments of slowly clip-clopping through the silent hedge-lined lanes and then excitedly trotting into a vast open expanse of wilderness to discover the never-ending views across the golden bracken hillsides, woodlands, heaths and green pastured valleys. My little grey Aladdin stopped, pricked his ears, and started neighing out in greeting to the curious wild ponies around us, with Lisa's Merlin quickly joining in. Even with cold, ruddy cheeks and socks which weren't quite keeping our toes warm enough, we were smiling with undiluted joy.

John, all of a sudden, kicked his beautiful steed, Copper, and raced to the top of a nearby hillock, where he defiantly reared up, claiming that he was king of the land. It felt like a big magical world, and that from the top, we had conquered it.

SCOOTER BOUND TO BORTH

The summer is coming to an end, but I know there were still maybe a few more weeks to grab of longish days with half-decent weather before Britain closes shop for the year.

"You don't understand. It's definitely not going to be on the big, heavy motorcycle. I'm tempted to just go off for a few spontaneous days. I want to take a slow, hassle free way up to Wales, and definitely without the motorways. I want to simplify it. Maybe just take a small backpack and jump on my scooter. It's old, I know, but damn reliable, light enough to pick up if it falls over, and really cost efficient on the fuel."

Lisa looks up from her cup of coffee and wisely nods, "It seems a long way from London on that little thing. But if you want to get onto some of those real small roads in mid-Wales, a smaller and lighter two-wheeler would definitely make life a lot easier. What takes your fancy?"

"I'm not really wanting to do much distance. Maybe come up through Hereford then do a loop up through to Borth, down the coast a bit, and back again. Do you remember those times going up there with Dad?"

Lisa smiles, "Like hell I do! Dad always liked taking us to Borth's sand dunes and seaside when we were small. Do you remember, with his gung ho attitude he'd allow us crazy kids to ride in the back of his grey Morris Minor pickup truck? We'd sit on the sides, on the wheel cases, and be battered by the wind!"

I can't help but laugh. "Yes I do! And he'd bang on the back window behind him as he drove through Hereford and the towns and villages of Wales ordering us to quickly get down and hide, in case the police caught us "illegally" sitting in the open back. It felt really naughty."

A week later packing my lovely old retro scooter, my black Aprilia Habana Custom 125cc, which had been ridden so much the mileometer had even stopped working, was a piece of cake.

I'd taken my soft fabric, bicycle pannier bags and simply swung them over the back of the seat, securing them down with elastic straps. The bare essentials were tightly packed in: just a change of clothes, warm woolly hat and gloves, toiletries, light waterproof jacket and trousers, and a few maps. I also left some room for sustenance and simple fare, like sandwiches and drinks I'd buy along the way. This meant I didn't need to take the rucksack. The only problem with that was every time the scooter needed filling up with petrol, as the cap was under the seat, I'd have to undo the straps and take the bags off. But fuel consumption, although with a fairly small fuel tank capacity of just 6.6 litres, was excellent. I'd been getting a reliable seventy to eighty-five miles per gallon running on supermarket petrol. But hey-ho, unpacking the scooter seemed like a trivial thing to worry about and, in my estimations, fillups would only cost about £6 each time! For extra storage and easier access to valuable items, like phone and money, I simply attached my big bum bag around the handles. Job done.

Again, due to the forecasted possible rainy weather in Wales over the next week and wanting to pack as little as possible, I'd decided to forgo the "camping experience" with sleeping bag and tent and opted to stay at Welsh hostels along the way. I'd found some pretty remote ones, and being on the lighter automatic scooter made me feel a lot more confident that I'd be able to take up the challenge in finding and then accessing these places, however steep, narrow, or windy the lanes or tracks were. The beauty with the scooter was that I could pick it up should it fall.

Although the "enjoyable" part of the trip was only starting when I left Hereford, I still needed to get there, which in my estimations was a good 140 miles away on the B roads from London. So early the next morning, on a crisp sunny September day after the 9 o'clock rush hour and with everything packed, I was off. I made my way up and around Heathrow on the minor roads, skirting the M25, now known as Britain's busiest motorway that some even call Britain's biggest car park, with its continual congestion.

I still had no real idea on the best route up to Hereford to avoid the motorways, as I normally only used the boring but quick M4 to Swindon then up through Cirencester, the Cotswolds, and Gloucester. Leaving leafy Walton and over the Thames, the choice was finally made to go up through Windsor, Eton College, Henley-on-Thames (for a cheeky coffee), past Oxford, and onto the A40. The day was dry and sunny and the four-stroke 125 engine was soon zipping me up to sixty miles per hour on the flat roads and, with a little encouragement approaching Cheltenham, got up to sixty-five, and then with the wind blowing in the right direction I amazingly reached seventy flat out. But I reckon that was a lucky one-off!

After slightly more than four hours and a slightly sore bum, the beautiful rolling green hills of my much beloved

Herefordshire welcomed me with open arms as I sped through Dymock, Little Marcle, Trumpet, Tarrington, Bartestree, the flooded Lugg Meadows, the Cock of Tupsley, and up into Hereford to my mother's home, with its views out to the cathedral and distant Welsh mountains.

The next morning, I leapt into mini survival mode or maybe just a cost cutting exercise! I generously buttered two thick slabs of rustic white bread with added Marmite, cheese, and pickle before wrapping them up in a bag with a couple of apples. Travel sustenance, saving money, and self-sufficiency were essential on this little expedition, and hopefully, I'll find a remote and picturesque country lay-by somewhere around lunchtime, before arriving at my planned destination close to Rhayader. Kisses were blown into the air as my mother waved me goodbye, repeating and shouting her mantra that I stay safe and eat well for the next five days. My smiling open-faced helmet nodded in total agreement and my gloved hand theatrically and royally waved goodbye as the fat little scooter wheels quickly sped off rolling down the hill into town.

Passing the old Victorian Somerville Hotel, our family home for over twenty years, I noticed it hadn't really changed since my parents ran it back in the 1960s and '70s. As children growing up there, we'd had some of the best times, running havoc with teenage parties in the cellars and earning pocket money changing beds and serving guests their dinner.

Traffic is always congested in Hereford. But warm memories came flooding back as I made my way through the town centre and passed the old Cattle and Livestock Market, now just another anonymous shopping mall and multi-screen cinema complex. It was only in 2011 that the market closed its doors forever and moved out of town, past the racecourse. But it was this marketplace that made Hereford such an important place in and around the Borders and was a natural hive of activity. As a small kid, I vividly remember looking forward to Wednesday Market Days, where we'd walk through the pens of sheep, ponies, pigs, and cattle before they were led into the ring to be sold. The strong, earthly smell of those animals bunched up closely together, avoiding or unknowingly treading through cow pats, and hearing those deafening animal noises was something like nowhere else. Old wizened farmers leaning on their crooks or herding sticks, with their black and white collies close to heel, would congregate in the bullring and stand or sit around it in anticipation. In a blink of an eye, the auctioneer would scream like a lunatic, shouting a million words a second, bang down his hammer, and the animals would be led out again into someone else's truck or pen.

For hundreds of years, Hereford life revolved around this market. It was the reason why people travelled there, not just from the villages and towns around the county, but also from across the Welsh and Worcestershire borders. Traditionally, on market day, farmers and their wives would come into the city to buy and sell their animals and produce and have a real day out, escaping from their hard-working lives on the land. Back in the day, it was a common sight to see traders juggling china, livestock drovers driving their flocks through the city, visits by the Queen, children playing in and around the empty market pens after hours, the happy crowds from Wales arriving for Miners' Fortnight, and stubborn grunting pigs standing their ground. It naturally became a hub for farmers to catch up on each other's news and the older ones to reminisce over a beer or two at the Old Market Inn in Newmarket Street.

Shortly past Eign Street junction, another Hereford landmark appeared of the massive metal woodpecker statue that stood for years at the entrance of Bulmers Cider Factory. This iconic 1960s' work of art had lately been moved across the road to take pride of place in the Cider Garden, which the cider giant gave as a gift "to the city and people of Hereford." In many ways, the woodpecker's new home is closer to its roots, now being just feet away from the original ciderworks established by Percy and Fred Bulmer back in 1888.

The mile-long tree-lined King's Acre Road led me slowly westwards out of town onto the A438, one of my favourite and most picturesque roads, which tightly hugs the slow meandering River Wye and meadows, passing the old river settlements of Breinton and its natural spring, Preston-on-Wye, Monnington-on-Wye, Bredwardine, the book capital of the world—Hay-on-Wye—and finally across the border into Talgarth, Powys. But well before Hay and the famous tiny wooden Grade II listed toll bridge dating back to the 1700s at Whitney-on-Wye, I indicated right and turned onto the minor A4111 to enter the area in North-West Herefordshire famous for its Black and White Villages.

I pootled along, enjoying the relaxed, slow feel to the journey and the comfortable familiarity of that lovely area. Just a few miles further on I entered Eardisley and scootered up the main street with its pretty cottages and gardens to Tram Square, named for the horse-drawn tramway from Brecon to Kingston that ran through there from 1818 until the coming of the railway. This was just the start of Herefordshire's "Black and White Village Trail" that leads you on a forty-mile loop to visit the medieval Leominster, Dilwyn, Weobley, Kinnerseley, Eardisley, Kington, Lyonshall, Pembridge, Eardisland, and Kingsland. With their hundreds of timber-framed buildings, black and white cottages, tea rooms, craft outlets, and country pubs serving local gastro fare, this is a lovely way to spend a day or more anytime of the year.

Although sorely tempted, the only detour I did make was down a hidden lane alongside the Tram Inn signed Woods Eaves. After about a mile and turning right at the stone chapel I got off and pushed the scooter up onto its stand next to a farm to look in awe at one of Herefordshire's most remarkable veteran trees, the 900 year old Great Oak. It stands majestically higher than anything else around it, and I just wondered at the stories it could tell. Continuing up and along the A4111 towards Kington, the road climbs several miles up to Kingswood Reservoir, and it's there the perfect lay-by appeared to eat the simple fare. Sitting on the grass and looking out over the quiet countryside, without another soul in sight, there was a fine view of the Herefordshire countryside to the east and a foretaste of the Radnorshire Hills westward. That one simple pleasure brought a smile to my face as I ate the last delicious morsels and crumpled the sandwich wrapping back into my bags. The helmet was pulled back on and the road continued northwards, passing the Small Breeds Farm and the Owl Centre, which keeps one of the finest collections in Europe.

Kington, on the English Welsh border and one of the five Herefordshire market towns, is clustered around an impressive church. And it's there where it's reputedly haunted by a black dog said to be Conan Doyle's inspiration for *The Hound of the Baskervilles*! Without thinking, I automatically turned left and took the familiar A44 westwards, where after half an hour later passing through green-hedged roads, I stopped for petrol and the little room at the famous bikers' café at Crossgates, near Llandrindod Wells—or just "Landod" to the locals—on the Powys and Radnorshire border. This is normally a mega meeting point for bikers and some say the real start to the quiet and exciting empty roads leading into mid-Wales, where crazy bikers will more than exceed sensible speeds. But it was only Tuesday so it was fairly quiet, besides just a few bikers casually drinking tea at the tables outside. Saturday and Sunday would be a totally different story if the weather was good.

It was less than eleven miles to my final destination, which is a little farmhouse hostel I'd found in the village of Saint Harmon, just outside Rhayader, which is recognised as the first town located closest to the beginning of the River Wye. But before finding my way there, I was sorely tempted to make just a slight three-mile detour on the B4518 to the spectacular dams and reservoirs of the Elan Valley. Hidden within the rolling Cambrian Mountains, that is one of my other favourite places in this remote part of beautiful Wales. I still have fond memories of that place when travelling with my father to the seaside town of Borth. Managed now by Welsh Water as a conservation area, The Elan Valley Reservoirs are a chain of man-made lakes, dams, and a seventy-three mile aqueduct originally built by the Birmingham Corporation Water Department in 1893 by damming the Elan and Claerwen rivers to supply desperately needed clean drinking water for Birmingham, in the West Midlands. Sadly, settlements and farming land within the valley were lost. Nowadays, the AA has ranked the Elan Valley as one of the Ten Top Roads in the World! The scenery is spectacular and a haven for wildlife and nature, with eighty miles of paths and trails for people to discover.

Whenever I go there, I feel at peace with the world. But right then, entering the Elan Estate and stopping at the Garreg-ddu Dam to look over its enormous water-filled reservoir, the skies had darkened, releasing drizzling rain. The light bicycling waterproof trousers were pulled out of the bag as a matter of urgency and quickly pulled on over the jeans. I continued just a bit further through the fir-lined hills to the next reservoir at Pengarreg Dam, where I know the Penbont House would be open for a traditional Welsh Afternoon Tea. The fireplace welcomed me, and I snuggled up close to it and warmed my hands with a cup of tea while savouring a slice of buttered Bara Brith and a Welsh cake drizzling with hot melted butter.

After the light rain had somewhat stopped, the scooter took me back along the silent, motionless grey and black bracken-lined lakes to Rhayader, where the only place still open to stock up for a meal that night was the local newsagents. A can of Heinz Cream of Tomato Soup and a crusty loaf of bread made me more than happy! The three-mile ride up to Saint Harmon on the tiny B4518 took me higher and higher into the hills, until the directions instructed me to pass through an old metal gate to Woodhouse Farm. I untied the old fraying string to open the heavy gate, lifted it to swing it back, rode through, got off the bike, repeated the exercise to close the gate, and then it was a long "bump up and down" ride along a rough pebbly track. The welcoming Mid Wales Bunkhouse appeared in the diminishing light, and unloading my bags, I found I'd be the only one who'd be occupying the twelve-bed bunk room that night! You could say I had the place to myself.

There was absolutely no need to rush the next morning, but with the constant chirping of countryside birds outside and a ray of sunshine coming through the crack in the curtains, I jumped off the bunk bed and took a further look through the window to assess how the day was looking. Across the rural surroundings, the sky was a washed-out blue with high, wispy clouds and no sign of imminent rain. That alone made me smile.

Another short journey that day—up towards the southern reaches of the Snowdonia National Park to explore some of the smaller tracks along the way would be wonderful. The sunny weather was holding as I emerged from the farm and onto the little B4518. But already across the road there was an even smaller and narrower lane which looked like it ascended and disappeared into the emerald green hills. That unmarked track would finally get somewhere close to the 473 metre high mountain summit of Dyrysgol. I spontaneously turned off onto it and, within a few moments, had climbed steeply and found, round a blind corner, the most spectacular view of a lost and hidden magical valley with a tiny stream flowing down along it at the bottom of the tall bracken-covered hillsides. I wheeled the scooter onto the lush green grass and, sitting down, breathed in the deep serenity of the place. With the lightness of the scooter it was a doddle to walk and turn it round the narrow pathway and ride safely back down the hill. Call me whatever, but that's not something I would have wanted to venture doing with the big weight of the motorcycle I'd left back in London.

With a metaphorical spring in my step from what I'd just discovered, I swung left back onto the B4518 and continued up through the countryside, reaching Llanidloes within the boundaries of Montgomeryshire. This pretty place, known as one of the great little market towns of Mid Wales, was also the first town on the upper reaches of the River Severn.

Just a few miles further north along the B4518 there was another 360-degree jaw-dropping stopping point at Llyn Clywedog reservoir. I sat down and pulled out some of the bread from the night before and a chocolate bar. It's in that part of the Cambrian Mountains of Mid Wales that the sources and beginnings of the two great Rivers Severn and Wye can be found on either side of the Hafren Forest. Both start at Plynlimon. The Severn, Britain's longest river, begins its journey in a deep, blanket-peat bog 610 metres above sea level, while the Wye is another watery oozing from another nearby bog in the same hillsides. Good sturdy walking boots are a must for this highly recommended twelve and a half mile moderate circular walk (www.wyewalker.com) with panoramic views and opportunities to see lots of birds, including jays, heron, buzzards, kestrels, pied wagtails, and chaffinches.

The road came to a little T-junction at the village of Llanbrynmair and turned left guiding me towards Machynlleth, Powys. On that sunny Wednesday, as I enter that beautiful little town, the Machynlleth market on the main street, with its overflowing tables of homemade jams, chutneys, fruit, and vegetables was well underway. This is maybe one of my favourite places in the area, and attracts alternative life-stylers from far and wide and has become the green capital of Wales, thanks mainly to the Centre of Alternative Technology just up the road. It was also in a little shepherd's dwelling nearby, where Robert Plant spent his childhood, and that Led Zeppelin escaped to and created some of their most iconic music in the early 1970s. Bron Yr Aur had neither running water nor mains electricity, but three months later they had written "Led Zeppelin III," an album so radically different that it would influence the rest of their career. It's even said that at the same time Jimmy Page began writing one of the band's most iconic songs, *Stairway to Heaven*.

Sitting outside one of the cafés on the lively main thoroughfare, I peacefully watched the hustle and bustle around me with the market store holders bartering with the locals, and out-of-towners peering through tempting shop windows and wandering into the local pubs. The final leg of the day's journey continued just three miles up through the rolling wooded hills on the A487 to the peaceful former slate village of Corris. I rode down into and through the silent village with its tiny cottages and up a narrow steep lane leading to the Old School, perhaps better known now as the bohemian Corris Hostel. Again, it's only with the scooter that I could have safely parked and heaved it onto its stand on such a steep incline. Walking through the peaceful terraced landscaped gardens with a few smiling faces looking at me, with their long hair and unconventional appearances, and then into a massive church-like room with a cosy wood fire, piles of books and games on tables, it felt more like a hippie commune. The welcome was perfect as I was led into a little dorm with just another girl and her dreadlocks sitting peacefully cross-legged on her bed. Nestled in the foothills of Cadair Idris, a large mountain at this southern end of the Snowdonia National Park, the place felt perfect to hang out for a couple of days.

My soul had been replenished with its meditation areas, good wholesome food from the communal kitchen, and beers in the evenings with fellow travellers exchanging stories around the large log camp fire.

Fortunately, the scooter hadn't slid down the steep lane while it had been parked up, and so, finally throwing the bags over and tying them down, I merrily twisted the throttle and was off again to the jolly songs of the morning birds and a guitar playing melodically from the hostel. The softly curving, fir-tree-lined empty road finally flattened out to a wide green valley floor and it's there I veered off onto the B4405 and entered the beautiful and enchanting countryside to ride alongside the narrow-gauge Talyllyn Railway, made famous as the inspiration of Reverend Wilbert Awdry's *Thomas the Tank Stories*. Contented, peaceful sheep and cows were gently grazing in the valley meadows as I passed serene lakes and signs for Dolgoch Falls. The terminal of the Talyllyn was just a few miles away at the coastal town of Tywyn with its long sandy beach.

The A493 road continued southbound, tightly hugging the coastline. What can I say? It was absolutely jaw-droppingly beautiful and even more so when the road reached the broad estuary of the River Dovey, curving round to reveal Aberdovey with its pretty pastel-coloured Georgian town houses. Unable to cross the estuary, the same road headed eastwards along the River Dovey Valley and back through Machynlleth, southbound onto the opposite side of the estuary and turned into the A487. That is now the main Welsh coastal road, which will ultimately go all the way south to Fishguard, with its passenger ferry services to Ireland.

It's true that the schools had gone back about a week ago after the summer holidays, but it was amazing not to see more campervans and traffic out on those roads, besides the occasional and obligatory tractor. The whole place seemed very much like I'd got it to myself, and even more so when I excitedly turned off at the petrol station T-junction and onto the B4353 towards Ynyslas's wild rolling sand dunes and bird sanctuary at the coast's very tip, close to Borth. There the view was sublime, overlooking the Dyfi Estuary to Aberdovey with distant views out to the mountains in Snowdonia.

Heaving the scooter up onto its stand and leaving it sheltered on the side of the sandy track, I wandered off across the wide expanse of flat tidal beach, where sea birds were pecking at the sand. Walking through the tall spiky grasses, I slid down the massive dunes to come out onto the three-mile stretch of white, soft Ynyslas Beach to face the strong breezes coming in from the Cardigan Bay. This is all part of the Dyfi National Nature Reserve, situated midway between Aberystwyth and Machynlleth. The views were spectacular from every direction you looked and once again, I was not surprised that I still found this one of the most beautiful places anywhere in the world! Just a few other people were there that day quietly walking along the sea's edge or wildly flying kites. I flopped down and rested my head against a dune and felt the soft tingling sand running through my fingers as the soft warm breeze and calm sound of the waves slowly invited me to close my eyes for a while—another simple pleasure. It amazed me that I'd only done forty-two miles that day; sixteen miles from Corris to Tywyn and then a further twenty-six miles here to Ynyslas and Borth. But the diversity for such a small place and the fact that it never changes is truly remarkable and one of the reasons why I found this place so special and always want to return.

Leaving the estuary, I passed Cors Fochno, a raised peat mire, which is part of the Dyfi Biosphere and, incredibly, the only UNESCO Biosphere reserve in Wales, and continued just a few more miles. As I closely hugged the coast, passing the windswept links Ynyslas Golf Club, with its hillocks of sandy grass dunes splattered throughout the fairways, and then past the odd caravan site, I entered the little seaside town of Borth. I turned into a driveway of a yellow painted Edwardian house that is now better known as the town's youth hostel. The old scooter had done me well that day. As I swung the bags off the seat and checked in to find out, once again, that I'd be the only "adventurous" guest staying, so the big bunk room was just for me.

Like so many holiday seaside resorts up and down the British coastline, Borth has probably seen better days, with its one main street lined with tightly hugging, somewhat shabby "one up—one down" homes on either side and in between them the odd tea house with the ever-present Chinese and Indian takeaways and the obligatory pub or two. But walking slowly further down the road with not much else to do, I happily noticed a little bit of re-vamping activity had been done with a trendy looking beach-like café—the Oriel Tir A

Mor Gallery—and a fantastic renovated arthouse cinema, the Libanus 1877. This made me happy that Borth was being re-energized, but whatever happens, it would always hold some of my warmest childhood memories.

Walking back to the hostel, I picked up some fish and chips and returned back along the beach. It was low tide by then, and an ancient submerged forest was visible where stumps of oak, pine, birch, willow, and hazel could be seen. Researchers have said and proven by radiocarbon dating that those trees died about 1500 BC and were incredibly preserved by the unique acid conditions in the surrounding peat. Truly amazing, as I munched on my vinegar splashed chips!

The salty sea sprayed bedroom window was showing promise the next day as rays of sunlight pierced through it. It was time to get back to Hereford, but not before heading a little further south along the coast to Aberystwyth and with a ride up into its remote neighbouring hills to stay overnight with my friend, Olly.

I opted to take the minor coastal B4572, and I was not disappointed. As I left and gradually climbed the steep green countryside hills, the views finally opened up at the top to totally overlook Borth, the long beaches, and the rippling sea way below. Then it was quickly downhill through the narrow country lanes into the much larger university town of Aberystwyth, with its pastel-hued Georgian houses lining the promenade and the flashing lights of amusement arcades twinkling from the pier. I rode to the very end, close to South Beach, to look back out along the promenade, which just a few weeks back would have had the bucket-and-spade brigades out in force. But this day it was very much quieter, except for the sound of the noisy screeching seagulls spiralling overhead. I turned the key, pressed the start button, and we were off again, through the town, and soon climbing once again the ever-narrowing roads and lanes, through forests, and finally into the tiny hamlet of Cwmerfyn, comprised of no more than half a dozen cute white painted and black slated cottages.

No doubt, hearing the noisy scooter coming up the lane and shattering the calm, the friendly, smiling face of Olly curiously appeared from her cottage. She waved and pointed to the little area close to her motorcycle where I could park up. Tea and excited non-stop chatter pursued, then stronger drinks and lovely food, followed with even more banter continuing late into the evening.

Olly finally sipped her last drop of wine from her glass. "We really must organize something together. You know, a little journey together on the bikes would be fun. I'm up for it."

I clapped my hands with glee and smiled knowingly. "Yes, that sounds like a cracker. Two girls on bikes out to cause mayhem! We'll need to have a good think about where we'd both like to go, but I've already been ruminating on a few ideas, which I think at least one may interest you! Let's make a plan sooner, rather than later!"

And with that I was leaving the next morning with ideas for a future escapade already in the planning stages! The ride eastwards, initially on the isolated narrow lanes through the sheep-lined fields high up in the hills from Cymerfyn, was sublime. Then it continued with the spectacular ride through the remote and empty mountain roads of the A44, following the infancy of the River Wye to Llangurig and then further south to Rhayader.

From then onwards I was in home territory and turned the faithful old scooter back towards The Borders and Hereford, twisting the throttle to accelerate and smiling as my little bicycle saddle bags began taking on a life of their own wildly flapping in the wind and wanting to fly away.

Chasing the Welsh Red Dragon

Solo Motorcycling around Wales

We were well into mid-summer, with those long, cherished sunny days and light finally disappearing into the late evening. People were spontaneously smiling in the streets, flip-flops and shorts had become the normal attire, and that evening the smell of mouth-watering BBQs wafted up and over the garden hedges. Hopefully that was an omen for continuing good weather over the next week. My bag was packed and my beloved Bonneville was parked up outside ready for the next day's extended journey.

The morning mist rising over the garden with the sun brightly starting to appear was sign enough that the day was off to a good start. The bike was loaded, and I was ready to leave the quietness of Hereford. But packing this bike, which was the first and only motorcycle that I had ever owned, was now a little more different than any other bike! Just six months earlier, the beautiful but ageing T100 790 cc Triumph Bonneville, with its original cream and racing green tank, had received a little re-vamp! A beautiful, brown leather café racer seat had been delivered to me from Los Angeles by British Customs to replace the original long, weather-beaten, and torn seat. And since then, with the help of a local friend, Alan, who knew a lot about adapting old classic bikes, the back fender and original seat had been removed and replaced by this new "one woman" seat with its curvy sloping back.

So just slinging my bag onto the back of the seat was no longer possible without it slipping off. As the bike was still my only form of transport and I was travelling almost every weekend to festivals with my books, I was in need of a solution. Three young metal engineers I'd met in London came to the rescue. They miraculously built a "one-off" customized floating metal tray that would be attached by side bolts and be suspended above the back part of the seat. So robust was this structure that I was able to carry a fairly hefty weight, but now being slightly top-heavy, manoeuvrability had become a compromise and agility had become somewhat hampered.

Incredibly, the tray was loaded and piled up with a bag of clothes, a sleeping bag, a tent, a floor mat, and a pop-up panel! All food and extras were crammed into fabric side bags that were attached and tied around the tray's metal side bars. The tank bag was filled with bits and bobs. The books had already been shipped to the two festivals I was going to visit in the coming weekends in Llangollen and Aberdare.

Today I was off up into northern Wales to Llangollen for their weekend motorcycle extravaganza, and the following weekend I was repeating the exercise, heading south to the historic Aberdare Races in the Welsh Valleys. It had seemed nonsensical to bike all the way back to London to just come back up a few days later. So, without much persuasion, I'd decided to spend that week in between in travelling and wandering around my beloved Wales and exploring some lesser known areas. Time was on my side; I had no need to rush, so here and now the aim was to ride up on some of the smaller, more picturesque roads along the Welsh Borders and venture around as much of the coast as possible before returning to the Valleys and Brecon Beacons.

The deep, sexy sound of the rumbling engine comes to life and before long is purring contentedly along the beautiful River Wye hugging A438, which penetrates deeper into the green countryside. Without even needing to look down at the folded map under the plastic pocket of the tank bag, I turn the bike northwards through the black and white village of Eardisley and head towards Kington. A bit further along the hedge-lined A44, I make a stop at Crossgates service station and the popular bikers' cafe for a double fill up—one for me and one for the bike! Although a working weekday Friday, there are a number of bikers soaking up the sun outside and no doubt gossiping and comparing the size of their engines.

Checking that everything is securely strapped down, I start my beautiful-sounding engine and smile from within my helmet, noticing that a few heads have curiously turned around. I indicate right and turn up onto one of my favourite stretches of roads in the Radnorshire-Powys area, the A483, which leads out over the hills to Newtown and Welshpool.

This is a high-intensity stretch of road that goes on for over twenty miles to Newtown, the largest town in Powys, lying on the River Severn. The smooth tarmac surface is brilliant, with miles of constant bends and sweeping corners but with lots of reassuring visibility. There are also decent amounts of straights, which means it can be ridden very quickly at over sixty miles per hour most of the way, with the tricky tight corners mostly surfaced with Shellgrip to improve skid resistance. Some bikers even describe it like a racetrack, and once they've blasted past any cars or caravans, they're then away. Although I don't see any police, and I certainly am not exceeding speed limits, there are plenty of places for them to hide out!

Getting to the very top of the hillside ridge before descending down to Newtown, with vast uninterrupted views of bracken moorland and sheep grazing on the roadside, I pull my helmet visor up and park up on the side of this beautiful silent road. I look out into the distance to the vast expanse of hills and fields, and a strange but wonderful sense of new found freedom goes through my body. I no longer have any commitment to the corporate world. Unexpected emotion wells up, and I sniff back a tear, knowing that it was only just last year, in 2015, that I had given my notice at my full-time workplace. I had no idea what I was going to do but, what I did know was that life was too short and that I needed to get out of the rat race. Still with a bit of a lump in my throat in what I'd achieved, I amusingly tell myself that this isn't such a bad commute to work!

Just before pulling away, I look up to see a couple of red kites hovering and swooping overhead. With a wingspan of almost six feet, they're a sight to behold but, up until fairly recently, had become almost extinct in Wales. But with serious conservation, they're now more widely seen and have even become the national bird of Wales!

The road steeply descends into the former mill town of Newtown and through the pretty countryside and rolling hills of Montgomeryshire to the handsome old market town of Welshpool.

For a while, the road teasingly takes me back into Shropshire, England, and past Oswestry, which then turns into the A5 before re-entering Wales and heading towards Llangollen. This last stretch of valley road is beautiful, following the River Dee and the impressive Pontcysyllte Aqueduct and Canal, which being the highest ever built, has been declared a UNESCO World Heritage Site. It's here you can either hike or take simple horse-drawn barges along the old tow-paths. Approaching the pretty little town of Llangollen nestled on the banks of the fast-flowing River Dee, I cross the old stone bridge and head up the hill to Llantysilio Abbey and Abbey Farm Campsite, where I'll be staying for the next few days. Unloading the bike, setting up the tent and taking off the "tray" with everything on it, I sit back on the bike and once again feel its nakedness and potential agility.

With no other opportunity during the weekend, due to the festival, I have that immediate urge to take the bike up for a spin to Horseshoe Pass, further up the narrow A542. The ride is exhilarating, turning around the tight bends with the zig-zagging road getting progressively higher and higher into the mountains. At the road's highest point of 1,368 feet is the long-established Ponderosa Cafe, which serves a warming brew before I head back down to the riverside campsite, with the derelict Abbey serving as a perfect backdrop.

The weekend whizzes by. Shoulders are rubbed with a multitude of people, with the highlight being an introduction and chat with silver-haired legend "Ago," who immediately puts his arms around me for yet another photo opportunity! Now in his 70s, he still has that Italian charisma and wicked smile for all who meet him and still holds the accolade as winning the most races ever! Giacomo "Ago" Agostini, motorcycle road racer, won in his time an incredible record of 122 Grand Prix wins and fifteen World Championship victories, with his last Senior TT win in 1972. In 2019 he would even have a museum created just for him in his hometown of Bergamo, Italy, to celebrate his unbeatable achievements. With the festival coming to a close, I'm approached by smiling Mike, the Mayor of Llangollen, who strangely has leather bike bags flung over his shoulders but is still wearing the mayor's decorative silver necklace! He's an avid Harley-Davidson rider and looks just that slightly bit jealous when I tell him what my plans are for the next few days!

Early the next morning, after a fairly late night listening to live jazz played at the Abbey next to the campsite, I pull up the zip and crawl out of the tent to look up smilingly at beautiful blue skies. The bike's packed, and I head out over the field, already stopping at the farmhouse tearoom for coffee and buns, with a few extra stuffed into my panniers! The AA's "4 miles to 1 inch Wales Road Map" is folded on the right area, stuffed into my tank bag, and I merrily set off down the descending lane into the early "not quite awake yet" Llangollen.

The A5 westbound valley road at this time of day is beautifully quiet, and I am passing fir tree-lined hills and fields dotted with sleepy sheep. Practically the only sound is my bike rumbling down these green-hedged roads. Before long at Betws-y-Coed, I look down at the map, realizing I've just entered the Snowdonia National Park, and at Capel Curig, turn left onto the A4086 for a further five miles. The landscape is already quickly changing to thick forests and ever steepening hillsides. With a much chillier feel in the air, I pull up the zip on my black leather jacket. It's then I veer right on a narrow road and enter the famous rugged Pass of Llanberis.

The grey crags soar high above the fringes of scree and boulders lying at the base of these enormous cliffs. Mount Snowdon, soaring 3,560 feet, the highest mountain in Wales and the highest point in the British Isles outside Scotland, is almost within spitting distance. This whole place has become a mecca for rock climbers, and there are already a few cars parked on the infrequent roadside parking bays, with ardent climbers enthusiastically pulling their boots on. Even George Mallory, British explorer and mountaineer who was a leading member of early expeditions to Mount Everest in the early 1920s, used this place as serious training grounds.

I can't help but stop at Pen Y Pass Café, at 1,168 feet, to take in this awesome scenery and can only imagine how busy this place will become later on in the day with buses, cars, campervans, and their eager visitors. But now, at least for the moment in this early morning, my only other company in the greatly appreciated warm roadside café is a handful of animated hikers adorned with rucksacks, gloves, hats, and walking sticks. Further on is Llanberis, famous for its nearby slate quarries and home of the little Snowden Mountain Railway that runs for just over four miles to the top of Snowden! Finally, having covered about thirty-seven spectacular miles through Snowdonia Park and now dropping back down to sea level, I ride into Caernarfon on the northern shores. Passing the fishing boats in Caernarfon Bay, I catch a glimpse of giant Caernarfon Castle, with its impressive grey fortress walls and towers overlooking the Menai Strait and over to Anglesey. Unbelievably, Wales has the most castles in one country than any other in the world, with William the Conqueror being the first to build them here.

Out of Caernarfon on the A487 southward for about five miles, I bear right onto the A499, heading for Pwllheli, and find myself now officially on the Llyn Peninsula. This fairly undeveloped and more remote region of north Wales, averaging eight miles in width and some twenty-five miles long, is like a green finger of land jutting out into the Irish Sea. Looking at it on maps over the years, I'd always thought it looked more like the horn coming out of a fantasy animal's head, which was the rest of Wales. The whole place is unmistakably beautiful, and there's pure joy in simply just riding slowly and enjoying every simple moment. But after fifteen miles, I carefully veer right onto the B4417 for Morfa Nefyn, owned in its entirety by the National Trust. I ride into the car park and look out to the little village sitting above the safe haven of a pretty curve of sandy beach. It's hard to believe that this was once a busy cargo, shipbuilding, and herring port. It was even considered in the early 1800s as a possible home for ferries to Ireland, but in 1839, the House of Commons gave that job to Holyhead in Anglesey.

Riding along the north Llyn coast, which hardly seems to have any settlements besides the odd sheep farm, I pass scalloped coves, beaches, and rocky cliffs, which gives that feeling of total isolation and that maybe I'm coming to the end of the world. Almost reaching the tip of the peninsula with the roads progressively getting increasingly narrower, on the small B4413 I start to follow signs to Aberdaron, which will tally up to an impressive total of thirty-four miles from when I left Caernarfon. It's truly amazing to see over such short distances how landscapes can change so dramatically.

Two miles short of the tip, I reach Aberdaron, which feels like an "ends-of-the-earth" kind of place, with its white washed cottages and ancient smuggler-looking inns near the calm waterfront. But it's from navigating through the relatively busy village and coming to abrupt stops, due to on-coming camper vans driving through these narrow roads, that twinges of anxiety start to build up. It's here I'm feeling the impact of the full weight of the loaded-up bike, being forced to navigate slowly up these incredibly steep and winding roads that lead around and out of the village. Balance and throttle skills are paramount to keep this heavy bike from simply falling over, which always remains a niggling thought in the back of my head!

Now for the first time, I'm heading east and out along the southern coast and starting to follow good signs for the former fishing town turned quaint holiday resort of Abersoch, where I've planned to stay overnight. Arriving on the outskirts, I'm greeted by a water inlet with lush, green grassy banks hosting colourful-hulled sailing boats that have toppled sideways due to the waters disappearing on the outward tide. Here, too, are stacks of colourful fishing buoys nestled in the grass between mounds of white daisies. There's even an old, rusty abandoned fishing boat now awkwardly leaning on its side, with the possiblilty of totally falling over. I continue out of town for about half a mile steadily climbing a hill until at the very top I reach farmyard gates. On the other side are fields looking spectacularly out and down to the village, the beach, and sea beyond. This is Penrhyn campsite, and without further to do, a grassy pitch beckons me at the top of the grassy slope, the engine is switched off, and I simply start unpacking with a view to pitch the tent sooner rather than later. The weather couldn't be better. Besides a few friendly kids kicking footballs around, I look happily out to a new view—a quiet, beautiful, coastal countryside with cows speckled over the green hillsides and boats bobbing far out to sea.

It's not long before my thoughts turn to finding something tempting to eat, like maybe some freshly caught Welsh fish. The boots are exchanged for flip-flops, and I wander down the steep hillside road into Abersoch. Delightful little gourmet cafés are in abundance, as well as the obligatory bucket and spade shops and excited children pulling their parents to the beach. After a lazy walk along the sandy beach, with the rippling water gently lapping its shores, I head back to take another look at that delicious menu I'd seen earlier in town. The meal doesn't seem quite so guilt-ridden, as later on I slowly have to walk all the way back up to the campsite. Finally, that evening with a paper cup of wine in one hand, I sit back on the grass next to the tent and watch the sun slowly set over the hillsides under an ever-reddening sky.

The faint sound of mooing cows very early the next morning stirs me from a happy, deep sleep inside the warmth of the tent. Peering out, the sea is sparkling from the increasing rays of sun that makes me smile, knowing I won't need to pull on my waterproofs. Or at least, not just yet! The start of a handful of morning rituals take place: walking over to the washing facilities and getting dressed preferring to stand upright instead of crouching in the tent, unpegging and rolling up the tent and sleeping bag, loading everything back onto the bike "tray," magnetizing the tank bag back on, and carefully folding the right piece of map into its plastic cover. Finally, after cleaning my cereal bowl with some kitchen roll and stuffing my rations back into my side bag, I think I'm done.

It's still early, and even the kids haven't come out from their tents to start kicking their ball. I always feel slightly guilty, starting the bike up so early in the morning and disrupting the silence around me, but once out of the campsite, I know that quietness will very quickly resume. The clouds are low, but with the mild air I have a confident feeling there's no imminent rain, and anyway, I'm only going a short distance to explore a little-known place and hopefully find a hot cup of something.

The more than pretty A499 coastal road leads me a couple of miles to the little village of Llanbedrog, known as a bit of an "Arty Place" with Wales's oldest public art galleries and also home to a wonderful beach. Very quickly I turn up a narrow private road and, in beautiful grounds, stop in front of a silent Victorian Gothic mansion, which has become a beautiful centre for the arts, housing vast collections of classic and contemporary pieces of art that all have a Welsh theme. It's better known as Oriel Plas Glyn-y-Weddw and is normally open to the public, with its little tea room overlooking the wooded grounds sloping down to the distant sea. There's no one else here, and it's easy to understand why. It's only just 8.30, and the doors won't open for another couple of hours. I sigh with a little bit of disappointment but am happily surprised when, looking up at the frontage, I see beautiful stained-glass windows.

With that, I turn the bike round and set off down the hill, heading back onto the silent main road while all the time soaking up the peaceful quietness all around me. Surely, after just another four miles down the road, there's got to be a place that will be open by the time I reach Pwllheli (pronounced something like "Poothl-heli"), the capital of the Llyn peninsula. With its harsh grey-looking façades alongside contrasting brightly coloured Victorian buildings all lining the main street, I park up outside a cream coloured church, "Festri Penlan."

Thankfully, a small café is pulling its blinds open, and a smiling girl behind the counter chirps up, "Bore da!" I reply with a smiling and reciprocal "Good morning," knowing only too well that in this area there's a lot more Celtic Welsh spoken than English. Back on the road, it turns into the A497, and after just a couple of miles, I enter and ride up a small coastal hillock into the small and pretty village of Criccieth, which is clustered around its magnificent hilltop castle with its two Welsh flags flapping proudly from its turrets. I swing my leg over the bike, pat it like a good little pet, and take a curious wander along the narrow streets, getting the distinct impression that this place is a lot smarter than other places I've ridden through. The Old Castle Bakery, with its delightful stained-glass windows of bakers pushing bread into the ovens, is unfortunately closed but must do a roaring trade in the summer. Beautiful and quaint little cottages line the streets down to the large sweeping sand-and-shingle beach. Out across the bay, in front of the white Art Deco Dylan's highly acclaimed beach-front restaurant, the clouds have now dropped down and almost totally covered the hills on the other side.

Heading back up the hill, and with the sea's cold breeze and black cloud covered sky, I pull my jacket collar up and over my chin while stuffing my hands into my trouser pockets. Pleasingly, it's still only mid-morning, so passing Porthmadog, I take a small detour onto the A498 and head back into central Snowdonia to the picture-postcard village of Beddgelert. Beautiful grey-stone pubs and white-washed homes flank a burbling river with a pretty little two arched stone bridge that takes you to an old church surrounded by green hills. Besides a few people casually walking into a souvenir shop with a giant dragon sculpture guarding its entrance, the place feels unusually quiet for a day in July. No doubt, later in the day, coaches and cars will be arriving with noisy crowds, so for the moment I smile with contentment.

Fortunately, leaving Beddgelert, I don't need to ride the same road back but take the optional and just as pretty A4085 that sweeps through wooded hillsides, parallel to the little narrow-gauge Ffestiniog railway. It finally leads back down towards the colourful Italianate "village" of Portmeirion, made famous by the British cult programme *The Prisoner* and now a bustling Welsh but tasteful Disney settlement. Skirting the southern fringes of Snowdonia Park, the A487 becomes ever narrower, and once again, part of a quiet, scenic countryside, with lush green fields and beautiful rolling hills appearing all around me. Before finally heading southwards to Barmouth, the remote village of Penrhyndeudraeth, close to the wild Dwyryd Estuary, comes into sight and almost disappears within a blink of an eye! In 1998 it apparently became the UK's first Networked Village offering Internet access to residents via radio technology. It's here I turn south onto the coastal-hugging A496 for Barmouth. The sandy shoreline and the magnificent Harlech Castle come into view. The road takes me up the windy road of Harlech village, where I park up by the castle entrance looking out to the sea and the estuary way, way below. It's probably true to say that none of Edward I's mighty coastal fortresses has a more spectacular setting. Harlech Castle crowns a sheer rocky crag overlooking the sandy dunes far beneath it. To add to the drama, the rugged peaks of Snowdonia rise as a backdrop. Against fierce competition with Conwy, Caernarfon, and Beaumaris (Anglesey), this is, in my opinion, the most spectacular setting for any castle in North Wales, with all four castles designated as a World Heritage Site. This thick grey-stone walled castle shrieks with natural defences, but an amazing pathway of 108 steps was built rising steeply up the rock face to allow the besieged defenders to be fed and watered by ship. Today, it's easier to access with a modern "floating" footbridge, which amazingly, now allows you to enter the castle to witness the incredible views out to sea.

As time goes on, the road becomes increasingly busy with caravan parks and holiday homes dotted along it as I finally reach the outskirts of Barmouth. It's then leading down a steep turning down to the seafront that I see an almost hidden sign for the Hendre Mynach Barmouth Caravan and Camping Park. At the last minute, I quickly indicate right and cross over to ride down what, in my opinion, is an incredibly steep road to the campsite. Caravans are parked up and nestled closely next to each other beside manicured hedges, and the whole place feels fairly busy. With just a tent and "small vehicle," I pay the minimal £18 for a grassy patch in the middle of the campsite, which looks like it's one of the last ones available. It's still teasingly not raining, so with what is now becoming the daily custom at the campsites, I take advantage of it by putting the tent up as quickly as possible before it rains or gets dark and then take a leisurely leg-stretching walk along the seafront into Barmouth.

Despite having a Blue Flag beach and the beautiful Mawddach Estuary on its doorstep, the seaside resort of Barmouth feels slightly faded and has become yet another typical seaside resort with the usual chip shops and dodgem cars. Fortunately, I bypass most of the brash neon-lit stuff and head into the oldest part of the town and around the quay, where I find a quiet little café overlooking the quiet harbour with some half-decent food. Handfuls of little sailing and motor boats are attached to floating buoys and are constantly bobbing up and down on the quiet, rippling water as I look out towards Barmouth Bridge.

I love Barmouth Bridge. The Grade II listed single-track wooden railway viaduct, almost half a mile in length and built in 1867 across the estuary, also has a pedestrian walkway alongside the railway line. Amazingly, it's the longest timber viaduct in Wales and one of the oldest in regular use in Britain. Besides a few stoic fishermen casting their rods out and over the sides of the bridge, today the place is beautifully quiet. And the walk all the way across to Fairbourne simply makes you feel like you're floating above the waters below.

That evening back at the campsite, and with the bike parked right in front of me, I lie back in the tent with a bottle of Chablis held between my legs. With my bare feet resting on the cool grass outside, I unscrew the top and take a long relaxing swig, smiling that I've had yet another simple but fulfilling day.

The next morning, after pulling the tent down and packing it up, I walk over to the campsite's office to take a little recce to assess the road heading back up onto the main junction into Barmouth. It's been worrying me ever since I arrived. I have to almost crane my neck up to appreciate the extreme steepness of this road leading out of this place. It scares me. With the abnormally excessive weight of everything piled high onto the bike, including my commercial pop-up panels and promotional items, I'm reluctant to load it up totally before setting off. It worries me that I just won't have the acceleration and balancing expertise to keep on or bravery to get to the top of the hill, and then with the additional task to immediately turn onto the busy main road.

Solutions. Solutions. Solutions. There are always solutions! I'll try and ride the bike up the hill with nothing loaded on it, in order to keep it as light as possible. Then, like a donkey, I'll just have to carry everything up myself before packing it all back onto the bike! I don't really care what anyone else thinks of what I'm doing. It doesn't bother me that they may think I'm stupid or incapable. It's only me that needs to make this work. I start the bike up, swing my leg over, and with the hand gently on the accelerator and in low gear, move forwards, quickly accelerating more and more up the steep incline without stopping until I reach the very top. I let out a deep breath of relief and lean the heavy bike precariously on its stand. I then walk down the hill to pick up my stuff and, by now panting, repeat it a few more times. The bike is once again fully loaded, and at the top of the hill I'm a very happy girl.

Today I'm excited knowing that I'll be covering a lot of beautiful and diverse countryside, rather than a lot of miles. The morning feels a little chilly as I ride through slumbering Barmouth and follow the road southwards for Dolgellau. But I won't be taking the normal route to get around the estuary. A good biking friend had advised me on doing something totally different, which was a perfect shortcut and would save about four miles than taking the main route via Dolgellau. About eight miles along and close to Pen-Y-Bryn, passing beautiful riverside fields and fir clad hillsides, there's a pretty old toll bridge on the right taking you over to Penmaenpool. Approaching it, I see its road surface is made entirely from old wooden planks with a little white hut on the other end of the bridge. Mist has come down onto the hillsides and the planks are damp, which may mean they're a little more slippery. The water is mirror still, quietly reflecting the blackish grey and white clouds, a bobbing yellow buoy, and a small sailing boat's turquoise hull and orange mast. I slowly ride onto the bridge, bump over the uneven surface, and arrive safely onto the other side without any mishaps.

A smiling old guy peers out of the little white cabin window, "Good morning to you. It's quiet here at the moment. A good time to cross over before the traffic arrives. That'll be fifty pence for you and the bike!" And with that, he wishes me well and waves me cheerily goodbye.

The A493 sticks tightly along the dramatic Mawddach Estuary before reaching the small settlement of Fairbourne, which in a blink of an eye is yet another place you'd probably just go past. But I do make a stop and notice the railway line that heads out over the estuary to Barmouth, the beautiful views all around me, and a tempting chippy which is, unsurprisingly, not yet open. And by the time I get back to the bike, the clouds are opening up and a glint of bright blue is breaking through.

And without exaggeration, along this wild coastal shoreline and cliffside stretch of the A493 close to Llwyngwril, anyone would think I was navigating the beautiful Highway 1 in California! Seagulls perch on old stone cliff walls, the ever-increasing blue sea crashes down below, and the perfect empty road twists and turns to reveal ever more thrilling scenes.

Nestled where the mountains meet the sea is the tiny but beautiful village of Llwyngwril. I'm astounded in witnessing something I'd never seen before, and with my inquisitive nature it leaves me with no other choice but to stop and investigate further. All along the roadsides, on the bridges, in people's gardens, tied around street lamps, and sitting or propped up on park benches are crocheted or knitted life-size animals, humans, and mystical creatures! Sheepdogs chasing sheep, knitted chickens sitting on the bridge, a giant scrambling over the bridge, a blonde mermaid coyly sitting on a bench selling crocheted local fruit and fish, a shepherd with his dog and sheep sitting on another village bench with his woollen scarf wrapped around his woollen body and a woollen hat covering his woollen moustached face, a woollen Scottish Highlander playing a woollen bagpipe under a real tree, and so the surprises go on and reveal themselves throughout the village.

All this spectacular woven theatre is thanks to the Llwyngwril Yarn Bombers who were set up in 2015 to help raise money and entice visitors to this beautiful local area. Yarn bombing is a type of graffiti or street art that employs colourful displays of knitted or crocheted yarn, instead of paint. I stand next to the giant clinging onto the bridge, and while looking down to the flowing river, an elderly couple approach me hand in hand.

Seeing my curiosity, they stop and smile. "We hope you like our village. We have a myth here in the village of a giant named Gwril who was married to a mermaid. It's said that he ruled and lived in our hill fort of Castell-y-Gaer, which is strangely surrounded by large standing stones. Him and his cousin, Giant Idris from the surrounding Cader Idris Mountain, would playfully throw rocks at each other, and that's how the standing stones were formed!"

Continuing on, the road pushes inland for a short while and metamorphizes back into luxuriant green pastureland and rolling hills close to Llanegryn. The remote grassy verges look like they've only just been cut, and with absolutely no other traffic, the beautiful, flat, slowly winding road simply disappears out to the furthest hills. The sound of birdsong and the rumbling engine seem to strangely go together quite harmoniously! With no rain, the ride is easy, and before I know it, the little seaside town of Tywyn on this Cardigan Bay coastline comes into sight. Riding through the town I catch sight of the beautiful post box red Magic Lantern Cinema, which oozing with cultural and social history, was built in 1893 as the town's Assembly Rooms.

It's now really starting to feel like the summer break as I ride down the coast, along long sweeping beaches and coming to beautiful Aberdovey, with its pretty pastel Georgian town houses. Children and parents, with their buckets and spades and rolled up windbreakers, are marching to the seafront. Large sandcastles with watery moats are being built, deckchairs are being placed in prime positions, and older men with rolled up trousers are marching along the water's edge. The sun's now coming out, and the waters sparkle, with the little boats bobbing up and down in the estuary and the beautiful hills rising up from the banks on the other side close to Ynyslas and Borth.

It's almost lunchtime, and with my stomach starting to rumble, I know just the place to head for! Around the last stretch of the A493 coastal road to lovely Machynlleth, which is probably the most cosmopolitan of the local towns with its little eateries and arty shops.

I'd also done a bit of research on something else incredibly interesting to do close by but have, frustratingly, missed the daily slot, which meant I wouldn't be riding further into the nearby mountains to sit on a hill slope to witness fighter jets flying just above me! The Mach Loop is a set of valleys, situated between Dolgellau in the north and Machynlleth in the south (and from which the Mach Loop gets its name) that are regularly used for tactical low-level flight training, with RAF military fighter jets flying as low as 100-250 feet (representing what pilots would fly in a combat scenario), which means that sitting on the hills you feel you can almost reach up to touch them. I'd looked up the

Operational Low Flying (OLF) RAF fast jets and Hercules aircraft training timetable on the Ministry of Defence's website, but frustratingly realise that today's viewing slot has been missed by a whisker.

Machynlleth is just on the edge of rural Powys, Wales's largest county and, in my humble opinion, one of the most beautiful, with its quiet market towns and an abundance of sheep and rolling green hills. Holidaymakers with kayaks in the back of their trucks are also filling up when I arrive at the town's only petrol station. Parking up on the main street, timing couldn't be better, as it's Market Day and all the stalls with their fresh fruit and vegetables are crammed up next to each other, while leading up to the impressive old octagonal town clock tower. It's sunny, and I've soon grabbed a stool and purple crate table outside Number Twenty One to indulge in some of their delicious and locally sourced Welsh food. Everyone seems to be smiling as I hungrily tuck into a hearty vegetable lasagne and watch the world go by.

A trip along the Welsh coast for me wouldn't be complete without taking a small detour to visit one of my favourite places just across the estuary. So back on the A487 heading to Aberystwyth and after just ten miles, I make a turn onto the little B4353 to Ynyslas Nature Reserve and Borth's giant sandy dunes. At the very end of this sand blown road, past all the holiday chalets and links golf course, the bike is switched off, and I walk out along the vast beach overlooking Aberdyfi. This place never ceases to amaze me with its pure natural beauty, its estuary brimming with wildlife, soaring mountains all around, grassy sand dune pathways leading enticingly to the sea, and long untouched beaches on the other side. Squawking seagulls are swooping overhead, and there are just a few four-by-four vehicles parked up on the hard sand, where the waters have receded back out to sea. Filled up with a new energy after a healthy invigorating walk, I bring the bike back to life and turn southwards towards the lively university and ancient market town of Aberystwyth.

After, literally, just a handful of miles, I'm already reversing and parking the bike up along the busy promenade to scout for an ice-cream and indulge in another leisurely walk. The bucket and spade families are out in force on the beach below, and the amusement arcades on the pier are doing excellent business with the happy-go-lucky holidaymakers. Smiling, I catch sight of "A Mr. Whippy" van parked up on the roadside and, after patiently waiting in the queue, walk away licking the soft creamy ice-cream, having not forgotten to ask for the two obligatory chocolate flakes!

Leaving Aberystwyth and the central and northerly rolling hills, the countryside gradually levels out, transforming into vast swathes of patch-work fields running parallel to the wave-bitten Celtic coast around Cardigan Bay. Just another sixteen miles on the A487, and I've easily found the campsite at Drefnewydd Farm, conveniently located next to the coastal pathway and just outside Aberaeron. The site is perfect for bikers, being totally level with spacious pitches right next to the beach. As I bump over the grass, I sense a friendly and relaxed atmosphere, with the other campers lazily whiling away the hours.

After a shower with endless hot water and feeling happy on the slow progress of the journey so far, I go out to stretch my legs along the coastal walkway and arrive at the beautiful harbourside town of Aberaeron. With the harbour almost drained, due to the outward tide, the boats are now precariously balancing on their hulls. But the impressive and brightly painted Georgian houses surrounding the harbour give this place a feel of stylish elegance. From the corner of my eye I curiously see a queue forming outside the orange wooden-clad wharf building of the Hive, famous for its honey ice-cream, and feel it would be wrong not to be part of it! A few moments later, walking along the streets lined with its pretty independent shops and chic cafés, I'm licking ice-cream heaven from my waffle cone. Ever the one easily led into decadent temptation, the evening continues in the same style, looking out at the boats at the hip Harbour Master waterfront restaurant while devouring succulent Cardigan Bay shellfish. As I convincingly tell myself, "It would be wrong not to treat yourself at least once on any sort of journey!"

After a while sitting on the beach at sunset, reality on my basic journey hits home when I return back to the campsite, squeeze into my one-man tent, put my head torch on to aimlessly search for toothpaste, and twist and slither out of my jeans before disappearing into my sleeping bag! Who ever said five-star hotels were the best!

Even with the imminent weather warnings for rain, luck is still my friend, as washed-out but sunny skies welcome me the next day, following an unbelievably good night's kip! Between here and Cardigan, which is only a measly twenty-three miles directly on the A487, biking friends had enthusiastically told me there were oodles of fantastic little detours I should definitely explore and that could quite easily take up a day! So that would work out well, as I was planning to stay in a remote place not too far away as my last night on the Welsh coast before heading back inland.

Riding out of the hillside campsite, I bumble down and out of Aberaeron and, within just a handful of miles southwards, have already turned the bike back towards the coast and down the small B4342 lane to New Quay. The place is probably better known for when Dylan Thomas and his young family lived there during the latter part of World War II and where, unsurprisingly, there are plenty of little haunts to visit, including his favourite pub, The Black Lion. New Quay also lays claim to being the fictional small Welsh fishing village, Llareggub, in Dylan's "Under Milk Wood." And on this early morning, plunging scarily down the little tumbling streets, riding down Glanmor Terrace with its pastel painted Victorian homes and past the silent cobbled little harbour, it evokes that quiet isolation and a time long gone by. Bottlenose dolphins are frequently seen frolicking near the harbour wall when the tide is up and the weather's calm. No doubt, the bog-standard cafés, beach bucket and spade shops, and obligatory pubs will open later and change the feel of the place. But for now at least, I'm happy to just twist and wind my way quietly through and head back out again.

Following the coast with impossibly narrow, hedgerow-hemmed lanes, hoping to God no big tractor or van will appear from the opposite direction, I'm led down to another gorgeous little bay at Llangrannog. But with the weight of the bike's luggage, it feels uneasily daunting to navigate down to this little village, which is wedged between the squeezed butts of two hills covered with the obligatory Welsh bracken and gorse. Fortunately, it's early, and stopping the bike for a while at the quiet seafront, I decide to carry on and reach my stop of the day. Aberporth the other small suggested detour, I'll miss riding down, and try, instead, to get to by walking along the Ceredigion Heritage Coastal Pathway once I've reached the relatively unknown little coastal hamlet of Mwnt.

Just five miles from Cardigan, I bump down the tiny lane to Mwnt revealing far below the coastal hilltops a beautiful and empty sandy horseshoe beach. Out in the fields close by is a tiny solitary white-washed church with a pyramid shaped hill as its backdrop. The little track continues to lead me to the isolated Blaenwaun Farm. Even in July the campsite, which is really only a big field, is almost totally empty. But what a field! It's at the highest point on the edge of the cliffside with views stretching out to the vast expanse of sea. The sandy beach and cliffs are under the custodianship of the National Trust. And incredibly, my little campsite is directly on the Ceredigion Heritage Pathway. It totals a beautiful sixty-three mile walk along a waymarked path between the mouths of the Rivers Teifi and Dovey. Today I am planning to walk just part of it to Aberporth and back.

I manage to get the bike close enough to the edge of the field to provide a one in a million uninterrupted view out to sea. With its windswept and refreshing solitude, I set about unpacking and pitching the tent. With that done, I simply walk across the field to check out the modern showers and washing facilities. Besides just two other vans parked up some distance away, we have the place all to ourselves, and I'm as happy as Larry! I'm glad I'd done a basic food shop of bread, sandwich fillers, and water yesterday in Aberaeron, as up here there's simply nothing besides the taste of the fresh air! Maybe I'll find something when I walk over to Aberporth.

Heavy clouds are starting to come in from the sea, but walking shoes are put on, and I set off along the beautiful, exhilarating coastal footpath, around the cliffs, through fields, woodlands, and finally down the little lane into the village of Aberporth with its two sandy sheltered beaches and rock pools now exposed at low tide. To top it all off, I find a friendly ice-cream van parked close to a life-sized leaping dolphin sculpture beautifully carved from Welsh oak. It's there I plonk myself down on the grass to indulge in just enjoying the summer sights and sounds around me. Swigging from my bottle of water, I finally feel refreshed enough to walk back up the steep hill and along the handful of miles of coastal path.

That evening, ever-darkening clouds are ominously drawing in, and I resign myself to the fact that tomorrow I'll no doubt be riding a lot of the way back through the Welsh Valleys in unpleasant but long overdue rain. Much later that night, the rain gently starts to patter onto the tent like little drumming fingers, and for that moment, I just sigh and pull the sleeping bag well over my head and roll over to sleep.

The little delicate fingers of rain have become more like the massive hands of heavy-weight boxers thumping and battering the tent as I reluctantly look out onto this miserable morning. I'm dreading the thought of packing a sodden tent. Scrambling inside the tent like a crazy ferret, I somehow pull my waterproof clothes on and pack my stuff up. Emerging with my helmet on, I'm met by a totally different landscape of low grey clouds covering the hills and with rain slashing in from the sea. The visor's pulled down to protect and keep me dry from the pouring rain, and finally with the tent folded away and bike loaded, I slowly manoeuvre out of the soggy field and navigate down the little lane.

With just one day left before getting to The Aberdare Races, I was originally going to continue down along the coast to enjoy Fishguard and St. Davids, then trundle down the south coast to Milford Haven and Tenby, before coming back up through Carmarthen. But the more than atrocious weather is forcing me to re-plan and take a shorter route to get to Aberdare, which I calculate is still over a hundred and twenty miles away! It's nearly always the same. The days with the longest mileage always seem to end up with the worst weather! If nothing else, the rain never did come during the rest of the week, so that in itself is pretty miraculous and something I don't take for granted.

So, for the next hour continually wiping my visor with my rain-soaked gloved hand, I just keep my head down guiding the bike carefully southwards on the A478 close to the Pembrokeshire National Park and finally onto the main eastbound A40 to Carmarthen. Normally, Carmarthen, which is the ancient capital of southwest Wales and apparently the birthplace of the wizard Merlin, is a lively market town. But today it's quickly bypassed on the anonymous A48. For the first time, it feels like I'm travelling with everybody else on a busy dual-carriageway, and with the slushing water coming up from the speeding lorries, the feeling's certainly not pleasant. Signs are beckoning me onto the M4 motorway to Swansea, where my godmother Sally once lived, and to the industrial sprawl of Port Talbot, famous for its massive steelworks. There's no way I want to mistakenly get onto that traffic-laden mayhem! So, as planned, it's here I diligently veer left and start riding through The Valleys.

Whenever I hear "The Valleys," my voice repeats it musically back in a Welsh up and down tone, adding "in The Valleys Boyo!" No other part of Wales is as instantly recognizable as The Valleys, which is a generic name for the string of settlements packed into the narrow cracks in the mountainous terrain to the north of Newport, Cardiff, and Swansea. The change from the rolling wild countryside I've just ridden through to this post-industrial landscape is almost immediate. Although it's much greener now, about three decades ago this place was still covered in slag heaps and soot-encrusted buildings, due to its dependence almost solely on coal mining. Britain was the world's first industrialized nation, and for more than a hundred years, South Wales, perhaps more than any other part of Britain, sacrificed so many lives and hardships by stoking more than 600 coal mines with the back-breaking toil of the miners. Almost every valley, with its working-class towns and rows of tiny coloured "one up-one down" terraced homes was dependent on coal. Men would work for unthinkably long hours in the pits and come home exhausted and black. Most homes had no bathrooms, so the wives would prepare hot water in buckets outside in the back yard for their men to wash, and then they'd dry beside the coal burning fireplaces inside.

Dignified memorials are found in almost every community to those who died underground. The most heart-rending case was in Aberfan with the catastrophic collapse of a colliery spoil tip in 1966. The tip had been created on the mountain slope above the village of Aberfan, near Merthyr Tydfil. That morning on 21 October, heavy rain had been unrelenting for weeks and led the tip to suddenly slide downhill, with the slurry ultimately killing 116 children and twenty-eight adults as it engulfed the local junior school and other buildings.

The BBC reported, "As the children left the coal-fire warmth of home they emerged into streets shrouded with a dense, cold fog. Mothers waved goodbye from the doorstep, never imagining in their worst nightmares that it would be for the last time. The 240 pupils of the Victorian red brick Pantglas Junior School wound their way through the gullies, the back lanes of the miners' terrace houses, crunching over layers of sodden clinker swept from the hearth and tipped there on a daily basis. As the children congregated for morning assembly, they were excited. At midday, the half-term holiday would begin.

"Their daily rendition of *All Things Bright and Beautiful*—a hymn written a few miles away in the bucolic tranquillity of the Usk Valley—was postponed that day. They would sing it before they went home when the head teacher planned to wish her pupils a safe and enjoyable holiday. Just moments later after 9 AM the school lights began to flicker and sway; an ominous roar like a jet plane screaming low over the school in the fog. The glistening black avalanche consumed rocks, trees, farm cottages then ruptured the Brecon Beacons to Cardiff water main, engorging it further and increasing the velocity of its murderous descent towards Pantglas. Muck began to harden and set like cement while torrents of dirty black flood water coursed into the village. The huge bank of water was coming towards the place like a terrifying tsunami. The crisis whistle sounded in the colliery and miners, with their headlamps still lit, ran to the school where women were clawing at the slurry with some who had no skin on their hands trying in vain to reach children who could be heard crying."

Nothing would ever be the same again after this cruel disaster with so many people forever traumatised by these living nightmares.

But The Valleys are stoic and no more so when I think about the Male Voice Choirs which also come alive in this part of Wales. Many a time I've heard them in a pub or patriotically singing during the rugby season. But it's here in The Valleys that they're the loudest and strongest, probably due to their hard-working roots when they would sing in the austere chapels, the miner's institutes, and drinking clubs. Throughout the fast moving and transformative nineteenth century industrialization in The Valleys, choirs of coal miners came together to praise God in the fervent way that was typical of the packed, poor communities. Classic hymns like *Cwm Rhondda* and the Welsh national anthem, *Hen Wlad Fy Nhadau* (*Land of My Fathers*), are synonymous with the choirs, whose full-blooded interpretations render all other efforts totally insipid.

And miraculously, with those deeply resonating choral sounds created in my mind, the rain's finally disappearing, leaving just dark grey but harmless skies. I pass through The Valley communities of Ammanford, Gwaun Cae Gurweni, Ystradgynlais (A4069, A4068, A4067), and Glynneath, all on the southern edges of the Brecon Beacons National Park and in some places giving tantalizing views out to these green wild hills and fields beyond. Looking down the sloping streets, there are row upon row of the little coloured terraced homes with cars tightly parked-up outside nose to nose.

Finally, and well before midday, I turn towards Aberdare on the A4059 and, minutes later passing yet more rows of terraced homes, have parked the bike outside Servini's Café on the high street. Authentic Italian coffee with a wide smile is served as I wander back outside to watch the world go by on this bustling Friday morning. Aberdare is another lively but sprawling valley town and has a unique offering. The Aberdare Races, annually welcoming professional and amateur racing motorcyclists for the weekend, takes place in the town's picturesque Victorian Park. The circular walkway surrounded by parkland will be turned into a serious racing track! Moments later, I'm riding the bike into the park, noticing the trees have already been surrounded by straw bales for their protection and for the safety of the riders with their speeding bikes who'll be battling for positions around the circuit tomorrow and Sunday.

Safely camped inside the park's enclosure with the other vendors, the sun shows its shining face over the weekend, and I'm honoured to sign books next to the legendary John McGuinness, famed for his record-breaking twenty-three wins at the Isle of Man TT Races. In his soft Lancashire accent, he even jokingly says my bike probably wouldn't be the best for racing the circuit, but he sits on my bike anyway—with me proudly sitting as his pillion—as cameras click, click, and click away! Speed and adrenalin are flowing throughout these next two days as enthusiastic crowds line the park cheering on the dare-devil competitors as they race towards the ever waving black and white chequered flag.

Aberdare Park feels like another world early on this Monday morning, as silence reigns with everything cleared away, besides just a few remaining vans loading racing bikes and packing to leave. The tent's religiously, for the last time, packed away, and the shining bike's chrome engine covers and exhaust pipes glimmer in the morning light. It'll be an entirely leisurely ride back to Hereford, opting to head through the Brecon Beacons on the mountainous A470 northwards from Merthyr Tydfil, rather than choosing the alternative route southwards through Abergavenny on the A465. It's only about sixty miles, and I'm riding to enjoy it.

The morning's fresh but clear as I twist up through the sleepy little streets of Aberdare and very soon reach the country roads and skim the Brecons on the A465 before heading in on the A470. Wildness greets me. Covering 520 square miles through Powys and Monmouthshire, the Brecon Beacons National Park has probably the lowest profile of Wales's three national parks, including Snowdonia and The Pembrokeshire Coast. But it's beautiful and a truly remote paradise. It's a land of red sandstone mountains, glacially-carved rock formations, castles, glass-like lakes, beautiful hills, green patchwork fields, and waterfalls hidden in ancient woodland, all part of a volcanic upheaval 500 million years ago. It's also home to Wales's first international dark-sky reserve for surreal stargazing opportunities.

The bike meanders up through the Brecons on the incredible A470, passing wild, tufted moorland cloaked by craggy slopes and hillsides. Remoter walks here are not for the fainthearted. The famous four to five hour 1,400 foot ascent "Gap" trail, which starts at the Neuadd reservoirs and makes a circuit around a ridge-top horseshoe of the Brecons, is used by the SAS for their secret endurance training. Nearby are also

Pen y Fan or Corn Du, the two highest peaks in south Wales, rising to 886 and 873 metres respectively above sea level.

At the northernmost tip, close to the farming market town of Brecon with its handsome Georgian buildings, I turn towards Llangorse village within the Black Mountains, forming the most easterly part of the Brecon Beacons. This whole area has a special place in my heart, as this is where I spent so much time as a child.

The habitual grazing sheep and Welsh mountain ponies are now never far away. This always feels like an only partly tamed place, with the soaring ridges that enclose its many secretive narrow valleys. The B4560 threads through rolling countryside to the massive reed-shored Llangorse Lake, just outside its namesake village. This is the largest natural lake in South Wales, formed all those millions of years ago by a glacier. On this quiet morning, little dinghies are sailing around, and a few solitary fishermen in their boats are casting their lines out for those elusive pike, bream, and eels.

From what I'd just experienced over the past week, it was clear to see that some of the best adventures and landscapes were simply just on my doorstep!

Deep in these beautiful Black Mountains before Talgarth, I slow down to pass the more-than-familiar little lost lane that wanders down to that hidden farm, which was once part of my childhood. I smile, remembering those magical times at Cwmfforest, and ride away with thoughts of galloping steeds and the never-ending freedom given to us in this wild, forgotten place.

PART THREE

Alba—Memories

Back in the early days of Britain's first package holidays abroad in the 1960s, my mother met another incredible woman. Her name was Betsy Scott, and she lived in the little village of Mugdock, just outside Glasgow. Her quiet, unassuming husband, Stuart, was a neurosurgeon at the Glasgow Royal Infirmary. Betsy was to become a lifelong friend to our whole family and unconsciously changed my outlook and perception of life for the better. As a rural retreat from Glasgow, Betsy and Stuart kept a small boat nestled on the "bonnie banks" of Loch Lomond that they would take out for weekends and extended holidays. They'd sail out to a little island in the middle of the loch that had just two tiny white cottages, one for the farmer's family and the other as their peaceful hideaway.

We were invited up on several occasions, with the adults living in the cottage and my sister and I sleeping excitedly on the boat. Experiencing Scotland like that for the first time, with that great expanse of water, the fir trees climbing the hillsides, the healthy fresh air, the mountains all around us, and the simplicity of everything gave us that feeling of total wild freedom. Days were unplanned and were spent diving off the boat, swimming in the loch, trying to water ski, patiently mastering rowing the little dinghy, painting the wooden boat's frame, collecting shells and stones on the shoreline, and eating outside and under the stars!

For some strange reason, there was an immediate bond between Betsy and me. Her penetrating, sparkling blue eyes, joyous smile, and positivity for life showed through in everything she did, which meant it was highly contagious. Although our age gap was significant, that was irrelevant, and our strong friendship developed and remained over the years until she passed away. She was certain we had known each other and been close in a previous life. She introduced me to spiritual awareness, reincarnation, and yoga and continually told me that this life is short and that we need to be kind and grab every moment.

One of her last letters is one I always keep close to me: "I have been encased in my little house for the last few days. I have never known such cold weather, deep snow and icy frosts here in Scotland. I was happy to sleep in my lounge on the couch wrapped in my duvet with a hot water bottle. Today it rains on the compressed snow but at least it's warmer and hopefully I shall be able to go for walks again. I think of you often and remember with pleasure the day we spent going around Hereford; you were a good guide and looked the part in your little knitted woollen hat. We ended up eating doughnuts in a small café. It's good to draw on those loving memories.

"Take it easy—do your yoga and meet those friends that will help and guide you. It's always a two-way thing you know;

I help you—you help me. Try not to have fear—it is the greatest hindrance in life (I have to fight this one very much). Enjoy your life's journey, it's all so interesting isn't it? I know you will do so well."

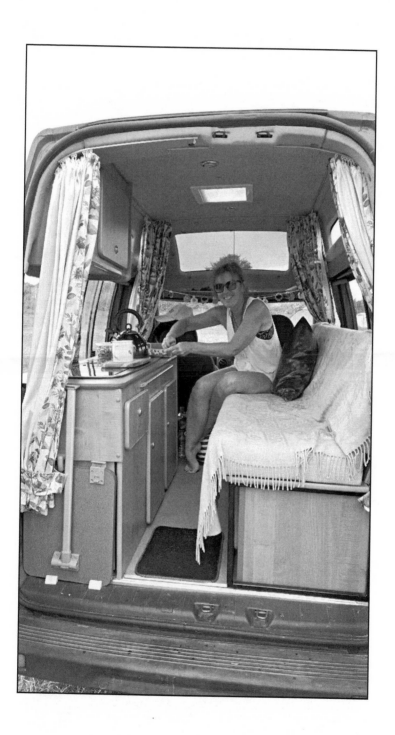

The Scottish Highlands and North Coast 500

Road Trip with Bernie, My Mini-Camper

Due to the increasing amount of merchandise I was taking to the summer festivals that was becoming harder and harder to pile on top of my newly customized Bonneville café racer and tiring of the weather-beaten tent, I needed to find an additional form of transport and accommodation.

A small, cheap van would do just the trick! But then I would also need to somehow find someone reliable, trustworthy, and obviously modestly priced to do the job to convert it into a little camper. I'd made contact with Rod just by chance in trawling the web for custom van builders, and with his wicked laughter, down to earth honesty, and good sense of humour, I felt by him the project would be done with care and without too much hassle. But finding a vehicle with fairly low mileage and with the scope to convert was more easily said than done. Finally, our painstaking and sometimes frustrating efforts paid off when Rod found a second-hand red Fiat Doblo 1.4 litre wheelchair van with that perfect high roof. And although more than fifteen years old, it had only done a measly 17,000 miles. Someone must have kept it in their garage unused for a very long time! I clapped my hands with glee and excitedly jumped on the train to the Bristol dealer and then drove the van all the way up on the M6 to Rod in Burnley, Lancashire.

Before leaving, and ever the one for a little bit of interior design and individuality, Rod duly complied with my wishes and drove us to Emanuel's, a curious and fascinating textile warehouse that had been converted from an old chapel. This was the perfect place to find some fabric for the van's curtains. And the place, run by English guys in the Asian area of Burnley, was certainly quirky and nothing I'd ever seen or experienced before.

Burnley knew all about fabrics, as it had been famous in the day for its cotton and textile production. Textiles had been made in that area since at least the Middle Ages, with the spinning and weaving of woollen cloth done by hand in the home. The growth of Burnley's textile industry was accompanied by the development of the engineering industry, particularly the manufacture of steam engines and looms. The area contained many foundries or ironworks supplying the cotton mills with machinery. And the town was also renowned in the day for its mill-engines, with the "Burnley Loom" recognised as one of the best in the world. By the 1880s Burnley was manufacturing more looms than any other place in the country. But the First World War had a serious effect on cotton manufacturers and signalled the start of a sad decline of the industry in Burnley. The war meant raw material was difficult to obtain; there was a shortage of manpower and many important markets were lost. After the war there was a short period of prosperity, but then came the slump of the 1920s and '30s. This led to massive unemployment and the collapse of many firms. Attempts were made to revive the industry through the introduction of new technology and types of cloth. But since the Second World War, competition from abroad and the use of man-made fibres sadly meant even further decline. Today Burnley, once the cotton weaving capital of the world, only has a handful of firms producing textiles. Nowadays, the place is probably better known for high-tech design and manufacturing companies supplying the aerospace industry.

We walk in to the chapel and Rod chirps up sounding like he knows what he's saying, "So this is how it's done. There's lots of rooms. All based on your budget. There's the £1 room over there with the cheapest rolls of fabrics at £1 a metre and then there's the £3, £4, and god forbid, the most expensive rooms, £5, £10 or more! Hopefully you won't need to go and see those! We're not fitting out Buckingham Palace!"

Unsurprisingly, the cheaper, synthetic fabrics in the £1 room aren't up my street in their designs or quality, and so with greater bravery and a frown from Rod, I finally step into the £5 room and immediately pounce on a lovely roll of perfect hippy chic fabric with massive flowers.

Over the next couple of months, being regularly updated, with Rod's due diligence the van is transformed into a proper little camper with a two-ring gas hob, a sink with water held in a plastic container underneath, a lovely fold-out double bed with comfy mattress and generous storage underneath, cupboards above and below the hob, lighting hooked up through a separate battery, and those colourful hippie curtains lining all the windows! Interestingly, Rod is also a serious sailor and so, from his practical knowledge, had created the fantastic cupboards like the ones you get on sailing yachts. With the click in and out buttons to open and shut them, it meant they'd never fly open when I went swerving round a country bend! No more cold meals or squashed food pulled out of my motorcycle's saddlebags, but the luxury of a stove to heat up or cook food and make hot drinks whenever and wherever it took my fancy. And that included finally being able to boil water for fresh coffee and decadently filling my hot water bottle on cold nights! With the added asset of also using the van as a place to shelter in from the unreliable British weather, it was in my opinion near perfect for any sort of distance travelling.

On the day I finally return back up to Burnley to pick up the finished van, Rod collects me from the station where we then plan to drive over to his workshop and where I'll be handed the keys. With his ever-smiling face, he turns and says in his strong northern accent, "We can't go to the workshop before you experience something from up here in the North! We're going to Haffner's in Burnley, famous around here for their delicious home-made pies!"

And true to his word, we drive into an industrial estate and through a fairly nondescript warehouse door, follow delicious smells to a counter crammed full with tantalizing pastry meat pies baked fresh on-site every day. Trading in Burnley since 1889, our eyes hungrily view Haffner's massive mouth-watering choices from beef and onion, pork and black pudding, meat and potato, steak and kidney, and cheese and onion. Laughing and hungrily eating our delicious pies back in his workshop, I'm finally given the keys.

Wiping his mouth from the flaky pastry, he swallows his last mouthful and says, "So now, what are you going to call your van? You do know, that most campers get a name!"

I rub my chin in thought then suddenly smile. "You know what? I've got the perfect name. I'm going to call it Bernie. I like the name, and it's apt, as it was created in Burnley!"

We both nod and laugh out loud with the play on words and shortly afterwards, with a bag of pies on my passenger seat to keep me company, I wave Rod goodbye and head back down south.

The following year, in 2019, at the beginning of September, there is still a window of opportunity providing a couple of weeks of forecasted good weather around the British Isles. Although not officially autumn for another week or so, the summer days are getting noticeably shorter and I still have that innate yearning to be back on the road. I decide this would be a fantastic opportunity to head up to Scotland, where I hadn't been for over thirty years! The drive would be leisurely, and hopefully, I'd navigate around the entire Highlands coastline and also follow the majority of the 500 mile-plus circular North Coast 500 route starting in Inverness and billed as Scotland's answer to "Route 66"! The idea is to stop along the way to see the sights and submerse myself into tartan, kilts, and whiskey.

The approximately ten-day plan and route is formulated in a casual enough way with a small Michelin pocket road map I'd found in a drawer at home, and soon childish excitement was growing inside me realising this would be my first extended trip in my little camper. A few days' provisions are bought, and bottles of water are stored carefully away under the seats. A thick, comfortable duvet and feather pillow with a cosy warm blanket are stored in the cupboard under the long seat in the back. Simplicity is the key to the journey, and the aim is to hopefully discover unexpected surprises along the way.

The usual congestion of the M1 heading northwards out of London very early that September morning is to be expected, and sitting back into the driver's seat, I content myself with singing along to Radio 2. That feeling of renewed freedom and being totally self-contained for the next few weeks feels very good!

The only issue, if I am not staying on campsites, is to find a place or two along the way to take a shower and wash behind my ears. My little camper, besides the sink, with its minimal fifteen-litre capacity container, has no wash facilities. But as I discover, that isn't really going to be a problem, as Scotland is fantastic in catering for the nomadic traveller. Washing and shower facilities are available throughout at the council pools, like Inverness at £1.50 a go; the marinas; railway stations, such as Fort William; the Fisherman's Mission in Mallaig, at £3.50 even including the towel; the Nairn Leisure Centre; the Assynt Leisure Centre in Lochinver; and The Hub Café in Ardgay at Bonar Bridge.

My aim today is to eat up the miles, head as far north as possible, and stop over at somewhere interesting before entering Scotland tomorrow. I'd never been to Northumberland but had heard many a story as to how wild and unspoilt this extreme northerly English county is, as well as having the accolade for one of the best beaches in Britain. So, the plan is to travel up close to the Scottish border to Bamburgh Castle, where this beach is located on this isolated eastern coast shoreline and stay there overnight. But before that, my first port of call after driving up the fairly nondescript 330 miles of anonymous motorways is a curious stop at Alnwick on the A1 to see something relatively unknown and peculiar with a maritime twist.

Parking Bernie up on the street and under some old trees, I walk along the quiet but pretty historic market town of Alnwick and enter the 300 year old coaching inn—The White Swan. Asking politely for directions at the reception desk, I'm pointed up some majestic red-carpeted stairs and enter the highly ornate Olympic Suite; a massive room furnished with the original interior oak carved panels and furnishings of the RMS *Olympic*, which was the relatively unknown but identical sister ship to the famous RMS *Titanic*! Both were built in Belfast by the White Star Line to compete in the burgeoning trans-Atlantic trade. On December 16, 1908, workers laid the keel for the White Star No. 400, to be called the *Olympic*. Three months later, No. 401—*Titanic*—followed on March 31, 1909. I'm the only person wandering curiously around in this silent but luxurious room and wonder how many people know about its existence. The room is laid out identically to how both ships' dining and lounge areas would have looked, even including the original ornate marble fireplaces and ostentatious crystal chandeliers! A man with a hoover and duster appears, and I quickly disappear back to the van.

Veering finally off the A1 eastwards, Northumberland's narrow country roads greet me until I can go no further, and I find myself looking out to sea at the pretty place of Seahouses, where a boat trip can take you out to the rocky Farne Islands to gawp at puffins and seals. It's then just a couple of lazy miles along the coast until I park alongside an empty road, walk through a wooden pedestrian gate, through some grass tufted sand dunes, and discover the most beautiful wild beach stretching out for miles in either direction. No wonder Bamburgh Beach has been nominated as the unequivocal best beach in Britain! Dominating the skyline on a grassy hillock and overlooking this vast expanse of pristine, windswept sandy shoreline is the breathtaking twelfth century Norman Bamburgh Castle. Once again, besides a few energetic walkers and their running dogs, I have the place all to myself. The little village just up the road, and also called Bamburgh, is quaint, to say the least, but has that unquestionable smell of money, with white-attired elderly people politely playing croquet on the manicured lawns outside the castle, people licking cones with homemade ice-cream, and posh cars parked up beside gastro pubs.

My place will be a little simpler tonight, the Budle Bay Campsite, just a few miles past the picturesque Budle Bay Estuary and impressive mud flats, which with its little viewing areas to stop and pull out binoculars, is a bird watchers paradise. I drive through the little countryside campsite gates and pull over. At £13 a night, I happily pay the smiling lodge owner, who thanks me with his strong London accent saying he'd escaped and moved here just a few years before. With unlimited choice, I park up onto the grass next to a little flowing stream. It's obviously the start of the quiet season, with all the caravans already empty and locked up. Following polite nods of acknowledgement, the only other camper is a Dutch girl on the other side of the field with a van so small I later see she needs to put a tent up alongside it. That evening after taking a warming hot shower in the Ladies Block, eating comforting pasta, and listening to the natural sounds around me, I smile with excitement that I'll be entering Scotland tomorrow.

Just thirteen miles further along the coast from the campsite the next morning, a warning sign indicates that it's only safe to cross the tidal causeway from 04.35 to 12.30. I look at my phone and smile with relief that there's still plenty of time to drive over to Holy Island and Lindisfarne Castle. And what a drive! Going out for miles, the watery, puddly, mudflats are on the same level as the now usable narrow road, with the sea waters receding far out into the bay. But in just four hours, at high tide, this same passageway will again become totally submerged, and anyone not respecting these signs will be stranded on Holy Island until the next low tide twelve hours later. Passing an unfortunate dead grey seal lying motionless in the grassy verges, the long straight road leads me to the island, which resembles a quaint old English village with post office, tea shops, and little stone cottages. The tourist buses have started to arrive as I walk down a quiet lane and, leaning over a gate, see over the field the remains of Lindisfarne Castle, built in 1550. At the time this castle was located in what was once the extremely volatile border area between England and Scotland. Not only did the English and Scots fight here, but the area was frequently attacked by Vikings from Scandinavia.

Driving back towards the causeway I wind my window down and breathe in the fresh, intoxicating air. This whole beautiful area of an ever-changing landscape of sand-dunes, mudflats, and coastline is the Lindisfarne National Nature Reserve and an important habitat for thousands of wintering waterfowl, who feed on the sea-grasses and marine creatures of these mudflats. Back in the summer these salt marshes would have burst into colour with flowers, including wild pink and purple marsh orchids. Jumping easily back onto the A1, I divert slightly over the historic Old Bridge, built in 1611, and into the northernmost town in England, the Anglo-Saxon settlement of Berwick-upon-Tweed, located just a few miles from the border.

I continue on not really knowing what to expect, which lights up and keeps alive my simple curiosity. The morning is bright and sunny with piercing blue skies. All of a sudden, I spontaneously pull into a lay-by next to a yellow trailer selling haggis, tattle scones, and belly busting breakfasts for the lorry and truck drivers parked up alongside. The sign on the trailer simply says, "Welcome to the Border," with English and Scottish flags flapping on either side. I look up next to this busy dual carriageway and see a humongous blue and white Scottish flag sign announcing "Welcome to Scotland." There's that feeling of excitement with the freedom and knowing the little escapade is now really beginning.

The most challenging part of navigation now will be not to miss the correct exits on these busy "difficult if you want to stop and look at a map" roads. A little bit like being a solo biker, a solo driver using only maps still has just as much pressure for accuracy on these unknown roads. Only in a car I don't need to write the key instructions on my hand like I've sometimes had to do when riding my motorcycle! Before arriving at Loch Lomond and the Trossachs, later on today, I'm adamant in making a slight detour to Falkirk, between Edinburgh and Glasgow, to witness something I believe will be quite spectacular next to the Forth and Clyde Canals. Frowning with concentration down at the map, I mark with a pen what, in my opinion, is the easiest route.

Jumping back into the van, I turn the radio on, now hearing welcoming Scottish accents, and head towards Edinburgh on the A1, jump onto the M8 towards Glasgow, then veer onto the M9 and off at exit 5. Signs are already directing me to The Helix, a new parkland project with The Kelpies. Turning the ignition off, I look out across and alongside the long, narrow canal to see an incredible sight of two giant metal horse-head sculptures. They become even bigger as I walk towards them, and I am staggered by the beauty of these gigantic horses stretching thirty metres into the sky, with each weighing a massive 300 tonnes. The beautiful sculptures, designed by Glaswegian Andy Scott and only completed in 2013, depict kelpies, or water spirits, with a salute to the horse-powered heritage across Scotland. It's the heavy horses of Scottish industry and economy that pulled the wagons, ploughs, barges, and coal ships that shaped this Falkirk area on the River Forth.

It's only past Stirling, known as the Gateway to the Highlands with its iconic Castle on the rocky outcrop, that I finally get off the frantic motorway. The calmer countryside of the Trossachs, with its thickly forested hills and pretty winding roads, quickly appears. Here the Lowlands meet the Highlands of the north and west in an area rich in history thanks to Rob Roy, a real-life eighteenth century Highlander, cattle dealer and outlaw who became a Scottish folk hero akin to England's Robin Hood. Surrounded by the lilac and purple heather-clad hills, I head down the A873 and onto the A81 to the attractive village of Balmaha on Loch Lomond's less frequented eastern shoreline, where little white-hulled boats bob quietly on the loch's surface. It's hard to believe that this seemingly unspoilt place is just an hour's drive from bustling Edinburgh and Glasgow!

The light's starting to fade, and darkening clouds will very soon be turning into a slow, constant drizzle. But at the same time, a spectacular large ray of mystical golden light pours down from one of the clouds onto the hills on the other side of the loch, which makes the place feel quite magical. But I still need to find the campsite, which had been described as being in a very remote area. I continue further up the eastern shoreline, knowing it to be the quietest part of the loch, and pass Millarochy Bay, with its pretty views across the water and surrounding hills, until the road is almost no more and there's only the Cashel campsite.

It's another quiet and attractive place, sheltered in the forest by fir trees and located directly on the waterfront with only a few very hardened campers pitched up. The weather's getting evermore blustery, and there's no way I want to park right up to the water's edge with the little waves racing in. So, a better shelter is found near a hedge, which will hopefully protect little Bernie from being battered by the ever-increasing winds. And with that, I climb over the driver's seat, pull up the lid of the stove, press the button to ignite the flaming ring, fill my purple kettle with water, and within a few minutes I'm cosily drinking a hot cup of tea in the moderate warmth of the van, while safely looking out to the blustery landscapes outside and all around me.

It's good to be back on the shores of Loch Lomond after all those years as a child, and putting my cagoul on and pulling its hood over my head, I jump out of the back of the van and take a brisk walk along its windy shores. Nothing significant seems to have changed, and I'd forgotten how enormous this expanse of water is. Scotland is obviously famous for its lochs, but Loch Lomond is the largest lake anywhere in mainland Britain, covering a staggering twenty-four miles in length and 620 feet at its deepest point. Back in the van, after a hearty bowl of tomato soup, I pull out the bed, throwing the big warm duvet and sheepskin throw over it. With the sound of the whistling wind outside and hugging my hot water bottle, I have no doubt that there couldn't be a cosier place to sleep than where I currently am.

Twitching the curtains to look outside the next morning, the grey charcoal skies are leaking rain onto the empty and silent campsite. Rain is splattering the windows. Looking out and over to Loch Lomond, its waters are the same dark grey colour, with the mountains covered in low-lying, misty clouds. There's nothing more to do but to fold the bed away, brush my teeth, and make a warming brew before looking at the maps for the next leg of the journey.

Oh, the joy of the empty roads early in the morning. Besides the occasional squeaky sound of the windscreen wipers, it's a silent drive through the Victorian resort of Balloch, through Alexandria on the southern most tip of the loch, and over the River Leven. Heading directly northwards, the road becomes the A82, hugging the entire western shoreline of Loch Lomond. It's here that it starts to feel more commercial and something I can't remember seeing all those years ago, with throngs of holiday homes, campsites, and hotels obscuring and taking over the view of the loch.

Just a little further on, I turn into a little country road and pass a field of woolly ginger Highland cattle with their long fringes and large curving horns. The long-haired outer layer of their coat is oily and repels rain and snow, keeping the fluffier undercoat dry and toasty against their skin. They've been bred through natural selection—only the fittest survived—in the wet and windy Scottish Highlands. They're also the oldest registered cattle breed in the world. Farmers used to keep their Highland cattle in open-air stone shelters called folds, and that name stuck—a group of Highlanders is uniquely called a fold, not a herd.

Shortly, I park up outside the Luss village newspaper shop and post office. A visit to Loch Lomond wouldn't be complete without sending a postcard of its picturesque views back to my mother and taking back an obligatory box of Scottish shortbread biscuits to hopefully shake her memory, which is gradually, and tragically, being lost by Alzheimers.

Skirting the shores of Loch Lomond and almost reaching its northern tip, I pull into an empty car park and walk across the road to The Drovers, the epitome of an historic eighteenth century Highland inn and sanctuary for walkers. It was once, many moons ago, a place of shelter for the Highland drovers driving their cattle south. On this misty morning there's just one or two hardy rucksack-laden walkers, stoically waiting outside to maybe venture along the woodland walk to Rob Roy's Bathtub, also known as the Falls of Falloch, and a couple of Americans clad in unflattering yellow fluorescent cagouls and oversized shorts. I enter this atmospheric darkened place with its low ceilings and am met by an old stuffed bear standing on its hind legs. There seem to be ancient stuffed animals and birds occupying every possible space, but the bare stone floors, open fireplaces with roaring flames, cosy darkened alcoves, and welcoming bars make it feel like a place of sanctuary.

But I continue on, now entering the mountainous Central Highlands of Argyll and Bute, until the temptation is there once again to stop just outside the isolated Bridge of Orchy village overlooking misty Loch Tulla. The sign clearly says, "No motorhomes—7AM—7PM", but I reckon little Bernie isn't a space-taking giant and more like a car, so the notice and lack of police on duty doesn't worry me in the slightest in flouting the rules. I'm glad I'd named my little van Bernie, due to the fact that it had undertaken its flattering, plastic enhancing surgery in Burnley near Preston. A cup is brewed on the stove, and I smile, reckoning this must be the best place with the best view serving fresh coffee! The vistas are now opening up, and it's now I feel, at least for me, I'm reaching the unknown and never explored.

Soon afterwards, I enter magical Glen Coe, and for the next half hour or so, I'm simply left speechless with its unexpected, mesmerizing beauty and majestic grandeur. It is a vision I had often dreamed of as representing the iconic image of the Highlands of Scotland but not thinking it existed in such magnitude. The quietness with nobody else here is creating excitement. *Glen* is the term for a narrow valley, and this is Scotland's most famous glen and, without doubt, the grandest— something you can only imagine, with maybe a mystical large antlered deer proudly standing and overlooking the glen to complete the picture. The approach to the glen from the east leads over the Pass of Glencoe, with its luxurious green and golden bracken covered mountainsides and into a narrow upper valley. This is where three massive, brooding spurs, known as The Three Sisters, dominate the glen. The tiny road winding its lonely way through the valley is so small in comparison to the giant mountains around it that it literally disappears and melts into the distant landscape. The passage follows deep gorges and crashing waterfalls emerging from the mountainsides until finally coming out to the more pastoral and calmer lower reaches of the glen and Glencoe Village.

There's happily and simply nothing else to do except to continue tightly hugging the wild green shoreline along Loch Linnhe. Passing Fort William on the busy mini-dual carriageway, instead of diverting the few extra miles to tick the box in seeing the highest mountain in Scotland and the British Isles—Ben Nevis—it's here I make a westward detour out and along the A830. The valley road is pretty, with its sloping fir tree-lined hills, but what I do notice between the hedges is a railway track running parallel alongside me. This line carries the famous Jacobite Steam Train, which leaves Fort William to travel a scenic two-hour run to the coast at Mallaig, which is by many classed unarguably as one of the great railway journeys of the world. One of the reasons it's rated so highly is because it also crosses the dramatic Glenfinnan Viaduct that was made famous in the *Harry Potter* films. The weather is thankfully clearing, but as I drive past, I unsurprisingly see the congested car park that I'd need to pay for in order to then walk across the fields to get a closer look at the Viaduct. Without hesitation, I go up a gear and simply look back at it in the rear-view mirror. The views from the van will do just nicely. The road then starts to open up until at Lochailort the rippling quiet waters on my left side appear again with unseen before views out to distant shorelines and remote islands.

Driving through the little village of Arisaig, I'm drawn to the beauty of the outer islands and, without a thought, come to a stop. I pull up on the roadside overlooking the sea and wander into a discreet beachfront café, taking my cup of freshly brewed coffee outside to a little patio. On the table next to me are a smiling couple, well, actually a sailor and his wife. In a thick Scottish accent, Tom chirps up, "There's a warm front coming in; you'll be lucky for at least the next few days. You can't beat the Isle of Skye this time of the year, now most of the campervans have left, and we thoroughly recommend driving all the way to Mallaig. Hopefully, you should be there when the steam train from Fort William arrives, and you might even be lucky enough to catch a boat and see some of the wild birds and dolphins."

I nod, mentally remembering these facts, and wave these kind people goodbye. The unspoilt beauty continues on along the last handful of miles of coastal road, with its inlets and gorgeous sandy beaches with clear views now across the sea to Eigg and Rhum. Through a wooden five-bar gate, I bump down a sandy track leading secretly to the beautiful Camusdarach Beach and adjoining campsite. Without much of a surprise, walking down to the old white-washed farmhouse to check in, I see that, once again, I'm almost the only guest staying, besides another caravan with a young family and a dog. The uninterrupted views out to sea from the field's campsite, perched on a grassy hilltop, are incredible. Once I've driven the van onto the gravel floored pitch and connected the van to the mains for electricity, I kick off my shoes, grab a towel, and head down the sandy pathway opening up to a virgin, silver-sand beach backed by dunes and machair grasslands.

Looking out to the Isle of Skye, in the Inner Hebrides, the wild, lonely beach with only the sounds of the crashing waves and the gusting wind is spectacular. The only other noises are the black and white seagulls circling and crying out high above. Apparently, fans of *Local Hero* make pilgrimages here, as this was the remote beach featured in that Scottish film. The day has warmed up, as Tom the sailor forecasted, and I lazily lie down, resting my head against a sand dune, and peacefully close my eyes, absorbing the warmth and serene sounds of the ebb and flow of the sea.

A white Scottie dog suddenly scuttles down a sand bank barking and chasing a thrown stick, and that moment tranquillity has momentarily disappeared. Later that evening, with a sweater wrapped around my shoulders, I cosily sit outside next to the van and witness a spectacular red "Shepherds Delight" sunset, with the sky's red, orange, blue, and purple shades intensifying then dimming out to sea as the sun finally disappears under its blanket for the night. And this is all tonic for a perfect night's sleep in the simple comfort of my cosy van.

The next morning the sun has thrown its blanket off and woken up again, with signs of bright blue skies that the day will be good again. The drive along the coast to the bustling fishing and ferry port of Mallaig is beautiful driving alongside small beaches and seaweed strewn inlets. True to my friends' words in Arisaig, it's not long before I start to hear the puffing sound of an enormous locomotive, and then I see it running parallel to me higher up in the grassy, heather-strewn slopes with the holidaymakers enthusiastically waving down from the windows. The train's already in Mallaig Station, panting with steam around it, by the time I arrive, and the van's parked up opposite in a public car park, as I take a wander over to take a little look. Steam train aficionados are lining the street and grassy verges enthusiastically taking photographs of the historic Jacobite Steam Train and, no doubt, waiting to witness its return back to Fort William.

Mallaig is a quaint little town known as a good base for taking day trips by ferry to the Small Isles, a small archipelago of islands in the Inner Hebrides, which are within spitting distance of this west coast, including Eigg and Rhum. Trips are also made across the waters to Skye. Walking to the little fishing harbour, I notice a beautiful and traditional sixty-five foot wooden vessel is offering short outings to hopefully catch glimpses of dolphins and maybe even some minke whales. Without hesitation, I hand my money over and, shortly afterwards, find myself boarding MV *Western Isles*, which was originally built for the Admiralty to deliver supplies to the large Navy ships at sea.

The skies are pristine and blue as we set off, with just a handful of other curious and smiling people, while passing fishing boats and quickly slipping into the Sound of Sleat between Mallaig and the Isle of Skye. It's a true fact told by our captain that Scotland has over 700 islands, including groups called Orkney, Shetland, and the Hebrides. And although he also convincingly tells us the west coast of Scotland is thriving with wildlife and we may well catch a glimpse of hillside deer or golden eagles soaring above and marine life ranging from gannets, puffins, Arctic terns, guillemots, basking sharks, dolphins, seals, and minke whales today, we're not in luck. Most birds have migrated away for the season. But that doesn't worry me. The very essence and enjoyment of being out to sea on a robust boat with the sunny skies and the wild wind and salty mist spraying playfully onto us is pleasure enough. The captain soon approaches us with a cheeky smile on his face and pours us wee drams of delicious, warming Nevis Dew Scotch Whisky. Without questioning, the glasses are filled again, and we all smile merrily back to shore. Jumping off the boat, I head to the Fish Market Restaurant, next to the harbour, for a plate of freshly caught Mallaig haddock in breadcrumbs and thick golden chips, which makes the visit to Mallaig more than perfect!

That afternoon I once again walk bare-footed along Camusdarach Beach, and incredibly as the only companion, a solitary eagle hovers overhead, following me along the water's edge. I stop sadly to see on this pristine, wild beach a washed-up plastic wine container. Being alone here feels as though there's even more responsibility to take action, so without a second thought, I pick it up and walk back through the dunes to also salvage and take away a couple of pieces of plastic fishing rope that had got stuck in the seaweed. With the sea's currents, I was just hoping that this beautiful place wouldn't become just another plastic-strewn beach, like so many other places around the world.

The long overdue rain had finally come in, pouring down relentlessly during the night, and the previously clear vistas have now totally disappeared under the dark rain-packed clouds. It is the perfect time to leave and head eastwards to officially start the North Coast 500, a spectacular 516 mile route around the coast of Scotland, normally starting in Inverness, the capital of the Highlands. Better known as the NC500, it was launched in 2015 by the Scottish Tourist Board as a touring route of the north Highlands, mainly following the coast and going through small villages and rural areas in this sparsely populated part of Scotland. My plan is to drive the majority of it, with possibly some detours, anti-clockwise, and finish up on the dramatic west coast and the Isle of Skye.

Driving back along the same coastal stretch of the A830, past the Glenfinnan Viaduct and to the intersection at Fort William, it's here I turn north-eastwards onto the wild A82 towards the iconic shores of Loch Ness. With the wind-screen wipers working overtime, and leaning forward, due to little visibility, I all of a sudden and unexpectedly jam my foot down on the brake to stop behind a stationery line of cars that have come out of nowhere and are waiting at a red light. This is the Caledonian Canal Bridge that will take us across the water to Fort Augustus and onto the western shores of Loch Ness. We'll just have to wait until the boats have passed. The sixty-mile Caledonian Canal, with twenty-nine locks, and built in the early nineteenth century by Scottish engineer Thomas Telford, connects the Scottish east coast at Inverness with the west coast at Corpach near Fort William. Finally, the lights turn green, and the cars, mostly with bicycles attached to them, accelerate off and have, thankfully, very soon disappeared out of sight. Reaching Fort Augustus, at the southern tip of Loch Ness, traffic to some degree seems to have built up again. But the views along this dark, deep, and narrow loch extending twenty-three miles in length exudes that ominous feeling that there may just be a monster lurking somewhere in its depths! Better known as "Nessie," the Loch Ness Monster is iconic in every sense with everybody, from enthusiastic amateurs to serious scientific teams, having scoured and explored its waters for this strange and mysterious creature.

One of the first stories of its sighting was back in the 1930s when a couple from London believed they'd sighted something: "It was horrible, an abomination. About fifty yards ahead, we saw an undulating sort of neck, and quickly followed by a large, ponderous body. I estimated the length to be twenty-five to thirty feet, its colour was a dark elephant grey. It crossed the road in a series of jerks, but because of the slope, we could not see its limbs. Although I accelerated quickly towards it, it had disappeared into the loch by the time I reached the spot. There was no sign of it in the water. I am a temperate man, but I am willing to take any oath that we saw this Loch Ness beast. I am certain that this creature was of a prehistoric species."

And it's created quite an industry here as I approach and park up outside Fort Augustus, watching cruise boats tackling the choppy waters and gift shops galore selling shelf-loads of "Nessie" memorabilia to appease the monster madness. My Scottish trip wouldn't be complete without also purchasing a souvenir, so returning back to the van, I tie a cute woollen sheep with long dangling legs and a tartan scarf onto my rear-view mirror. With its rolling-back button eyes, looking like it's totally exasperated in being taken on my trip, I can't help but smile.

Although I'm also incredibly vigilant, there's absolutely no sighting of the Loch Ness Monster today in this pouring rain, so I continue to Urquhart Castle, which commands a prime location on the banks of Loch Ness. Built between the thirteenth and sixteenth centuries, it played a pivotal role in the Wars of Scottish Independence in the fourteenth century and was later held as a royal castle. But the coaches have materialized, and the place is heaving with camera and umbrella wielding and waterproof clad tourists slowly queuing to enter the castle grounds or bustling into the huge visitor centre and gift shop. Call it impatience or not wanting to dosh out the money, but entering its inner sanctum is something I'm happy to refrain from, and after looking up at this medieval wonder, I decide to make a head start away from the giant coaches.

I am getting excited almost reaching Inverness and now the official start of the NC500. As Jeremy Clarkson had quite openly stated, "Route 66? Forget it! NC500 is the best drive in the world!"

Having hardly left the busy ring road around the relatively urban area of Inverness, and then crossing the Kessock Bridge over the Moray Firth, I've already decided to make an inquisitive detour. I am curious to take a closer look and discover the relatively unknown Black Isle east of Inverness, which is a peninsula rather than an island. So veering eastwards on the A832 country road and past Munlochy, I'm greeted by a surprisingly very different landscape of blackberry-hedged, gentle rolling fields, all looking out to sea and which have just been newly harvested. Giant circular bales of golden straw standing upright on these naked shorn fields are dotted throughout this countryside landscape.

Fortunately, the rain has decided to subside somewhat as I find the campsite at Fortrose, but it's now the wind I need to contend with. Without joking, this has to be one of the most unprotected campsites I've ever visited, and right next to the stormy sea. At reception, I'm strictly told to park in front of my allocated pitch number and, due to fire regulations, to keep six metres from my neighbour. My boundary is strictly between the blue and white posts. I almost salute to attention! Correctly parked up and making a hot drink, which thankfully also warms up the van's metal inside a bit, I feel the van already shuddering from the battering wind coming directly in from the sea and innocently hope it won't get knocked over or blown away!

The main reason I'd come here was because it was within walking distance of Chanonry Point, made famous for its bottlenose dolphins. Without a doubt, it's normally one of the best spots in the UK to view them throughout the year, particularly on an incoming tide, when they play and fish in the strong currents. The spit of sand and gravel running out into the Inverness Firth means that dolphins may be only metres away. I'll take the gamble. I wrap up with layers of sweaters and waterproofs and step out into the strong, gale like winds, the gusts almost knocking me over. Walking past the windblown and deserted Fortrose and Rosemarkie Links Golf Course, I finally reach the desolate Chanonry Point. Stormy waves are aggressively bashing the stony shores, so it seems that the chances of sighting dolphins will be zero.

Walking despondently back and rubbing my hands from the chill, I can't imagine being cooped up in the cold van for the rest of the day. After all, it's only early afternoon. I need to make contingency plans, and investigate to see if there's something interesting going on in Black Isle and away from this abysmal weather. I pack the little kettle away, jump back over into the driver's seat, and head out through the countryside to the pretty village of Cromarty at the very north-eastern tip of Black Isle. Upon arriving, I leave the van up a little side street and walk along the narrow, main street dotted with lovely eighteenth century red-sandstone houses and look out for the one attraction I'd found trawling my phone for anything remotely interesting to do in the area.

The village hall, with its triangular roof looking more like a church, comes into sight, and I eagerly walk in. Today it's open for a few hours, selling local produce and homemade goodies. Old men are chatting away behind jam and chutney filled tables, women are knitting and crocheting socks and scarves, natural smelling soaps are wafting my way, while the local fish monger is selling freshly caught scallops, crab, prawns, and fish. People are already starting to pack away, but not before I've bought a fully prepared cooked crab for supper tonight, spicy chutney, fresh bread, and a couple of bars of lavender and sweet orange soaps.

I wander on aimlessly through the quiet rain-sodden streets until I reach the small harbour on the other side of the town overlooking the Cromarty Firth and stand back, opening my eyes in total disbelief of the unexpected. Out in this beautiful sheltered area of sea are massive oil and gas rig platforms standing like sleeping monsters or aliens from another planet. Apparently, this is a place where the rigs are parked when not in use or when they're undergoing refurbishment. The price of crude oil is steadily declining, and in Scotland this means the abandonment of oil rigs. To disassemble the machines is not just costly, it also might prove to be a mistake, should the markets rise again. So, the massive rigs, weighing about a thousand tons each, are towed here from the North Sea. And it's in this bay that they're piling up and rusting until the economy turns.

But even in 2018, official figures showed that North Sea oil and gas production produced sales of £24 billion, an annual increase of thirty per cent and still supporting a whopping 269,000 jobs in Britain. Since oil was first discovered in 1966, and when full production started ten years later, the North Sea was found to have the largest oil resources in the European Union. But all that has to change over the next twenty-five years if an influential think tank's £170 billion green new deal plan is sanctioned, which means extraction would be phased out. But most people here like to think it's just a car park and not a cemetery.

The angry, unforgiving winds that continued to batter the van during the night have not yet let up when I wake up early the next morning. But at least I wasn't swept into the Moray Firth! Today's the start of seriously clocking up the miles around the first part of the NC500, which closely follows the eastern coastline. From the many articles I'd read, it sounded that this would be a lot less spectacular than the western Scottish coastline, but I didn't want to believe everything! And anyway, there was definitely one place I wanted to stop off at before reaching the extreme northern tip of John o' Groats.

Passing Helmsdale, a once booming herring port, the area soon transforms into jagged gorse-and-grass topped cliffs looking out to sea. This top corner of Scotland was once

Viking territory, and these cliffs still hide tiny fishing harbours. My small detour of the day is to visit Lybster, a tiny purpose-built fishing village dating from the early 1800s with its own pretty little harbour. The drive down from the main A9 road is extremely steep with serious bends down to this lost little place. Besides a couple of boats nestled in the harbour, a small gift shop, and café with its little museum on the fishing history of the place—having once been Scotland's third-busiest port—it feels definitely very sleepy. In fact, no one seems to be here, besides the friendly lady in the shop desperately trying to sell postcards and stories of the place. The sky has finally cleared, so after making a little brew in the van, I plonk myself down on a bench looking down to the harbour and hungrily eat a thickly cut sandwich to mull over the plan for the rest of the day. I notice the old "fish paths" circling the harbour's sloping sides that were once the routes used by the fisherfolk from other harbours to bring the herring catch to Lybster for curing. These have now become delightful walks around the coastline. It's only just past midday, so there's plenty of time to make one more brew!

The east coast continuing all the way up is fantastic, cutting through switchbacks and swooping valleys. Turning now into the A99, the coastal road continues up to the fairly nondescript Wick, once the world's largest fishing port for herring. But it's here, as a safety measure, I stop to fill up. I'd been told there really aren't a lot of petrol stations in the Highlands (even fewer are open 24/7) and to fill up whenever I could. Thinking about my bike back at home with its small tank range, this was a trip I'd definitely need to carry an emergency jerry can and potentially the bike would even be unusable here to complete such a trip!

The road heads further and further north to what feels like a more and more desolate and lonely place. There's very little seemingly happening here, with empty, gorse bitten land dotted with uninviting and isolated dwellings. But very soon the road has almost petered out. I come to a large, anonymous car park with hoards of caravans and cars, and flags and bunting flying everywhere, and people enthusiastically lining the road. Surely, they haven't come all this way to welcome me arriving at John o' Groats!

Coincidentally, I've just got here before hundreds of athletes are due to arrive, having just completed a marathon bicycle ride across Britain. And within minutes, the first athletic cyclists are maniacally pedalling to the finish line and receiving a rapturous welcome with medals flung over their helmeted heads. I walk away from the crowds and head towards the famous sign signifying it to be one of the furthest most points of Great Britain with Land's End's sister sign in Cornwall being 874 miles away. The northernmost point of the British mainland is actually Dunnet Head, where I'll be staying later in the day. Just below me on this rocky outcrop is a tiny little harbour with a couple of fishing boats and the John o' Groats passenger ferry getting ready to take people to Orkney. Besides a fairly modern but anonymous retail and unattractive catering complex on the other side of the car park, JOG isn't exactly a "must-see must-do" destination, and there really isn't any reason to stay any longer.

I have a yearning for something a little more cultural, which is exactly what I find just a handful of miles further up the road in Mey. I drive up a quaint hedge-lined country road and park up next to a high stone wall with an ornate green, garden gate leading into the Castle and Gardens of Mey. The turreted stone exterior of the castle is grand and imposing, with the proud Union Jack flying and flapping at full mast. But this isn't any old castle. This was home and retreat where the Queen Mother spent long periods of time after her husband, the former King George VI, passed away. Paying the "well worth it" £11, a handful of us walk inside with our kind guide, to a quaint little hallway with its hat and umbrella stands and original dog leads hung on the wall. Stairs lead up on both sides to the first floor, and it feels warm and welcoming—just like a normal home.

Everything is still in-situ, and we hear hilarious stories of the goings-on here while the Queen Mother resided here. One day, as a joke and during the summer, one of the housekeepers took a large ladder and placed small Santa Clauses and other similar comical props on the tops of mirrors and pictures all around the room. The consensus was to take them down well before the Queen Mother saw them, but the reaction from her couldn't have been better, and she loved the hilarity of it all, keeping them permanently there and using them as an ice-breaking talking point when visitors came to see her. The whole place feels so homely with the large airy and light sitting room, and its plumped up armchairs and sofas, quirky and comical memorabilia, a welcoming fireplace, hanging tapestries, and a writing desk with intimate family photographs. I smile when I see in the corner of the room a round drinks table with bottles of her favourite tipples: Gordon's Gin and Dubonnet with the obligatory slice of lemon. Amusingly, exactly what my mother has also always drank all her life.

Finally, I take a brisk walk around the beautiful walled garden with its flowers and vegetable plots before strolling across the immaculate lawns to take in the lovely views over the Pentland Firth. My place of residence tonight will be a little less majestic but, hopefully, with just as many mouth-watering views. Just a few miles further west is Dunnet Bay, offering one of Scotland's finest beaches and backed by giant undulating dunes.

I check into the massive Dunnet Bay Caravan and Motorhome Club Site. As a non-member of the club, I pay a premium of £26, which seems a lot and almost double what I've already paid at other campsites, but due to the beautiful location, I think I'm lucky to get a pitch in an already busy site. I haven't seen much wild camping yet, but maybe that's due to the fact that this is still a fairly well-frequented location.

Anyway, without further ado, I park up onto pitch 50, and immediately little Bernie feels like a dwarf next to all these monster-like, home-from-home vehicles, with some the size of buses or small bungalows! But the rain has thankfully stopped, and the sun is finally showing its face, and I'm just a hop, skip, and a jump from an enticing gate leading down to this most beautiful wide beach of creamy sand. Once again, besides just a handful of walkers and a few crazy kitesurfers leaping the foamy waves, the place feels almost empty. It's truly spectacular, and treading the pristine, untrodden sand, it feels like a "Robinson Crusoe" beach and I've been the first one to walk it all day. After a good hour's invigorating promenade, the light is quickly disappearing with the fading sun disappearing down into the sea. I'm feeling serenely contented, and I have nothing more to do but decide on what to eat from my well-stocked van's pantry and to plan for the next day's Scottish journey.

The giant campers are still asleep as Bernie creeps and bumps slowly over the grass and out of the campsite. It's then I put my foot down and head out onto the straight tarmac road heading westwards. The sun is greeting the sky, and the day looks optimistically good. From the rear view mirror, I catch glimpses of dramatic Dunnet Head, officially the most northerly point on the British mainland, and which beats John o' Groats hands down. The sand blown road with dunes on my right and a flat barren, blasted alien landscape on the other side reaches far out into the horizon. But no more than a mile further up, a public car park comes into view, where a solitary van has pitched up for a night of wild camping and is conveniently sheltered from the wind by the high sand dunes. Am I annoyed that I didn't know about it and that I'd forked out all that money last night? Not really, as there's nothing I can do now, but I do make a mental note of where it is for any future expedition.

I'm now officially driving along the very top of Scotland on the A836 and passing Thurso, Britain's most northerly mainland town and where without questioning how empty the tank is, I stop for petrol. Turning the key, I re-enter the wild, flat empty landscape with just the odd vehicle or two and tractor passing by. I'm curiously wondering if this far north can I even get radio reception. I switch my little radio on, and turning the knob back and forth finally tune into a local station. A friendly voice greets me reading the news and traffic conditions, which makes me giggle. "Please be aware drivers, that the only road delays at the moment are due to bales of hay out on the road leading to Achraemie!"

No more than twenty miles along this straight road with its increasing views out to sea, I turn off the A836 and up a tiny little lane, with only shy sheep nibbling the grassy roadsides as company. Strathy Point is, to say the least, very remote and home to the first lighthouse in Scotland, specifically built in the 1950s to be electrically operated. I arrive at an open gate that leads past a farmhouse, carefully reading the notice: "No Dogs! Please do not take your dog beyond this point. The cliffs are unfenced and sheep are liable to panic and go over the edge!" Just a little further, I'm given unrestricted views out to the now disused white lighthouse. With the sound of "baaaarrring" sheep, I get out and stretch my arms out and up to the sky, taking in and filling my lungs with the cleaner than clean wild air. The perfect tonic for an invigorating start to the day.

The westerly road quickly beckons me on. Towards Hope the spectacular purple heather and gorse moorlands with mounds of peat and crumbling dry stone dwellings give way in the far distance to the mountain ridges of Ben Hope. Thick cumulus clouds reveal a twisting and ornate tapestry around them of watery baby blue skies. And the further I drive, the more the road seems to teasingly curve and twist around this wild rocky coastline. It's not until I reach the crofting community of Bettyhill and cross a little estuary bridge that the land's flatness totally disappears, and once again, I'm met by the savage, rugged hills and mountains starting to dominate everything around them. With beautiful views of sandy beaches and offshore islands at Coldbackie, I reach Tongue and the ruins of Castle Varrich, to cross the causeway—an impressive feat of road engineering—going over the Kyle of Tongue Bay. Just outside the scattered village of Durness, a little sign politely indicates me into a small car park on the cliff's edge. Cars and campers are squashed in with a group of people walking around and looking enquiringly down to assess the steep drop down to the sea. This is the walking access point to get down to Smoo Cave which, with its vast entrance and river cascading through its roof, was apparently inhabited over 6,000 years ago! As is now usual, it's starting to drizzle, and there's a twinge of laziness in not risking my life in getting down the steep, slippery cliffside walkway. So, without a smidgen of guilt, I decide to give this one a miss.

The mission today is to try and find one of the most beautiful, isolated beaches as the next stop-over. Continuing southwards and now firmly following the westerly coast, I could have deviated to Sandwood Bay or Oldshoremore Beaches up the tiny B801. Both are famous for their beauty and remoteness, but I'm happy to continue driving until I cross the small stone arched Laxford Bridge to leave the A838 and take the smaller coastal hugging A394, which I'm soon to see becomes only wide enough for a couple of sheep or a brave small camper like Bernie! High up here, the views are mesmerizing looking over the inlet of Loch Laxford, with its little islands and famous for its bountiful, wild salmon fishing. In fact, the name *Laxford* derives from the Norse for "salmon fjord," so fishing must have been done here for a long, long time.

And with that thought of delicious salmon, I feel my stomach rumbling and know it's time for lunch and to find the place I knew wouldn't disappoint. Driving over the dramatic and beautiful Kylesku Bridge, designed by Ove Arup, who's the same person famous for creating the Sydney Opera House, I turn off and drive down a small steep road. Hidden from the main road, on the shores of Loch Glencoul, is the tiny hamlet of Kylesku. I park up and walk across the road to the award-winning Kylesku Hotel, overlooking the smallest of small piers and well-known in the area for serving up excellent seafood that's practically swum in through the door!—and that includes local mussels and other tasty fishy delights. I'm welcomed by a roaring log fire with just a couple of other people drinking up at the bar. I happily take a table overlooking the waters and very shortly am devouring locally landed "catch of the day" pan fried halibut fillet with crushed minted potatoes and local purple sprouting broccoli. Wiping the plate clean with a newly baked roll, I lean back in my chair and smile contentedly out to the bountiful, lapping waters.

Yet another small deviation, if that's at all possible, is made shortly afterwards at Unapool, where I head out again, encountering only sheep, and around the coast on the tortuous tiny single track B869, or Assynt coastal road, towards the remote crofting village of Drumbeg. This scenic link high-up between Kylesku and Lochinver, further south, passes dots of islands and strings of mussel farms, making it some of Scotland's most spectacular scenery. The bumpy track continues hugging rocky, grass covered hillsides where yet more curious sheep, maybe seeing my crazy-eyed sheep uncontrollably swinging from the mirror, clear the way for me to pass.

Finally, a bit further, after driving over 140 miles today, I turn onto an even unimaginablly smaller single track that provides a "sporting" recklessness in hanging on tightly from the bumps and ruts I'm driving over! But it's all worth it as I come around a corner to see a hidden turquoise blue sea, lined by a crystal white horseshoe beach. The sandy pathways leading through the low-lying grassy dunes to the empty beach are the definition of pure temptation. It's a bit of an exaggeration to call Achmelvich a village or even a settlement. It's actually a small campsite and caravan park. Shore Caravan Site also has a youth hostel attached to the owner's small house. There are no shops, besides a few sparsely stocked shelves behind the reception desk providing essentials, so you need to come stocked. I hand over one of those horrible, new slippery plastic £10 notes with three one-pound coins for a night's stay and head out over the bumpy grass to a little rocky promontory overlooking the receding lapping water below. The essential shower and toilet block is located within the centre of the field, but for the moment, this little bit of isolation will do me just fine in resting up and taking a walk down to the seashore.

With skies darkening far out on the horizon, with the omnipresent impending rain, I quickly gab the moment and step out to explore this beautiful and empty little place. I take off my shoes and walk along the beach, feeling the soft, pure white sand tickle and caress my bare feet. Another simple luxury that money just cannot buy. Later that afternoon before it gets dark, and thankfully with still no sign of rain, I simply park the van up on a vacant spot closer to the shower block for easier access the next morning. I'm feeling relaxed knowing in this quiet place I'll be able to nod off fairly easily tonight after a warm meal, cosily wrapped in my duvet in readiness for a fairly long, demanding trip tomorrow. The lights are turned off, I roll over, and slowly doze off. But this tranquillity doesn't last long!

In that pitch darkness, I hear the sound of vehicles approaching and, curiously looking out from the curtains, see two large rented camper vans from Perth have parked up right next to me! Why, in this empty field with all the empty space, would they want to park in such close proximity? No doubt, it must be due to the electrical sockets I reassuringly tell myself. I turn over and once again close my eyes. But not for long! A van door bangs shut, which startles me once again. The raucous sound of drunken people shouting and laughing and merrily jumping in and out of the vans is annoying, to say the least. With never-ending mouthy expletives, they don't sound like the sort of people who'd enjoy being told what to do or even to quieten down. So, with the non-stop sound of popping cans exploding beer and the noise getting increasingly louder, with music now turned up to full blast, it forces me to make sure all my doors are locked and that earplugs are firmly put in.

Almost before the sun has risen, I'm hurriedly putting away the bed, quietly pulling on clothes, using the washing facilities, and gulping down a hot coffee. Beer cans are strewn over the place, and heavy snoring can be heard from inside my neighbours' vans, so there's no real need for me to tip-toe.

Driving away through the fir-lined Inver Valley, the early morning sun's angelic rays flow through the clouds down onto the hazy hills on the horizon, and the darkness becomes light again. I open the window and rest my arm outside, feeling the fresh breeze as I pass Loch Assynt, with the ruined Ardvreck Castle standing on a rocky promontory of hillside within the lake. The weather doesn't really know what it's doing. In one moment, the skies have darkened and the lake has become theatrically black. Then in the next moment, snippets of blue sky appear and rays shine onto the rippling waters.

The southerly A837 turns into the A835 as it continues following the coastline to Ullapool, with fat, shorn sheep nibbling away everywhere I look. Somewhere here, in these mountainous roads and small hidden lochs, I hear the polite "beep beep" of a horn coming around the corner, and a cavalcade of classic cars suddenly appears slowly passing me from the other side. It's the Volvo Vintage Rally from the Netherlands!

I arrive at the pretty little port town of Ullapool in Ross-Shire, seeing on the map that it's diagonally opposite Inverness on the other coast, and admire its understated white-washed crofts and cottages nestled on the shores of Loch Broom. I park up and make a drink, taking the mug out to the shoreline to look out to the beautiful waters and surrounding hills noticing a large passenger boat is getting ready to head out to the Western Isles. Pulled up on the quiet shores is a four-man wooden skiff, no doubt previously used for fishing but probably now more for pleasure. This all brings back memories of the time I skiffed the entire length of the Thames, from its source in the Cotswolds to Greenwich, with three other hardy oarsmen! This place really was famous for its hardy rowers. So good were these boat people here that from 1870 to the 1930s it was known that the wealthy American aristocrats and self-made millionaires, like Lipton and the Vanderbilts, hired men from Broom Loch to leave for a year and crew their finest racing yachts.

And as men left these shores, others arrived! When the herring fishing stopped, mackerel appeared in these waters, and during the years of the Cold War 7,000 Russians came in their ships to buy the local fish! The friendly Communist visitors would come onto shore and got on so well with the locals that they'd exchange gifts. For about a decade, these ships would come to Ullapool, and they all got so friendly with each other that some of the village folk even helped the sailors source second-hand Lada cars to ship back to Russia. And that's not a red herring!

But red herrings do exist! Just opposite Ullapool, on Isle Martin, herrings were processed in the early 1800s. They would be smoked for three weeks and turn into dry, desiccated sticks of protein, which could then be sent to hot countries and, sadly, as nutritional food for slaves in the Caribbean. The term *red herring* also originates locally, with the pungent fish being dragged along a trail to train the young hunting hounds to follow a false scent!

Now well and truly in The Highlands, I set off again. The whole place feels so remote and impossibly more beautiful with each mile I cover; around the wild coastline, along Loch Maree, through the lost Glen Docherty valley with giant shale grass covered mountains and trickling life-giving streams. It's all just getting better and better. The little stretch of empty A896 or Glen Torridon Road close to Kinlochewe, and which winds spectacularly through a rich green mountain-lined valley with bubbling streams and a mottled blue sky, is a particularly special joy to behold.

The small, narrow road with fortunately little or no other traffic, continues to grip the coastline, swerving in and out around sharp bends, and finally comes out and around a little bay to the remote and delightful little village of Applecross. People are contentedly sitting outside the Applecross Inn drinking late afternoon beers with the view out to the Skye hills and the sea.

I drive up the steep hill to Applecross Campsite, which I'm pleased to see is within easy walking distance back to the pub, and without a problem, I'm offered a grassy green plot for just £9 overlooking the serene waters and village below. It's also here I swipe away the first midges I've encountered during the trip and rummage through the van to instantly spray on insect repellent, which had been advised was a necessity to bring along! Although Scotland is famous for its midges, up until now, I'd been incredibly lucky and hadn't seen or felt the little blighters! I pull on my walking boots and trudge back down the hill, through the village, and out along the narrow road leading onto and through the open moorlands. The air is invigorating, and I step up my pace so there'll be absolutely no guilt later on when I get that pint of beer pulled for me and tuck into some hearty, roasted venison at the Applecross Inn!

The next morning, I wipe the van's wet, misty windows and notice that with the clouds brushing the hills visibility will be very poor. I'm just a little disappointed, as the plan is to drive over Bealach na Ba, better known as the "Pass of the Cattle" and the only way to leave Appleby southwards. On a clear day the views way up there would have been incredible. In the olden days it was used to drive cattle from Applecross and surrounding settlements to other parts of the Highlands. It's known as the third-highest motor road in Great Britain with the longest continuous climb!

But with no other alternative route, I pack up and slowly drive out of Applecross and turn upwards to the pass. And I'm starting to see, even in the mist-shrouded hillsides, why this curvy mountainous road demands a hundred per cent concentration. It boasts in having the greatest ascent of any road climb in Britain, with an average gradient of twenty per cent! The hairpins are coiled on top of each other on an epic ascent, which climbs 2,054 feet in total over the course of just over five miles. It's certainly not for the sissies, with many bends perched over sheer drops, and it probably shouldn't be attempted by large vehicles or caravans, novice drivers or bikers or anyone who finds it difficult to reverse! The narrow, single-track road is similar to the great mountain passes in the Alps, with the tight hairpin bends switching back and forth up the hillside. No wonder Bealach na Ba has earned its fearsome reputation, and for many it's rightly considered the holy grail of British climbs.

Luckily, at this very early hour I'm the only one attempting the crossing, with the road so narrow that there are more than a few obligatory "passing places" for any unexpected, oncoming traffic. I'm concentrating desperately with the poor, almost zero visibility on keeping my eyes focused on the dangerous track ahead. It's then I reach a relatively flat piece of moorland with a passing place. I pull in, turn the engine off, and take a deep breath.

It's then from the nearby hillsides that I grab sight of a mysterious and ghostly shape emerging and walking slowly through the mist. A giant, antlered Red Stag appears and proudly stands motionless just a few feet away from me on these wild Scottish Highlands. Besides the sound of a small gurgling burn running down the hillside, there's total silence as we both stare curiously at each other. It's a truly mystical and magical moment. And with that, he shakes his head and slowly disappears back just as silently into the white foggy hillsides—the true vision of Scotland. So ironically, the lack of good weather with none of the long-distance views had given me something much better close-up here on Appleby Pass!

And amusingly, driving a little further on through Reraig Forest, I remember having contacted Colin Murdoch, who is based here and takes people on Highland Deer tracking walks but ironically had apologized, saying it was apparently the wrong time of year!

I was now heading towards the Isle of Skye in the Inner Hebrides, and instead of taking the shorter and easier option westwards on the A87 crossing over the third of a mile-long connecting bridge, built fairly recently in 1995, I'd decided to take an alternative and what I personally thought to be a much more interesting way of getting onto Skye! So, I continue to drive southwards on the same A87. But just past Dornie, on Loch Duich, stopping is again obligatory to gawp at maybe one of Scotland's most evocative sites. Eilean Donan Castle is set beautifully on an islet linked to the mainland by a little stone-arched bridge. But once more, the clouds are ominously blackening and droplets of rain can be heard hitting the van's roof like drumsticks. So, with a mug of tea and bowl of muesli, the view from inside the warm van is quite acceptable with the sound of the rhythmic rain.

From Eilean Donan Castle, the A87 continues to follow Loch Duich in spectacular Glen Shiel, with its soaring peaks on either side of the road. Just after ten o'clock, at what feels like it's a lot earlier due to these quiet desolate roads, a sign for Glenelg appears at Shiel Bridge, and smiling curiously, I turn down the misty and very windy narrow side road. Nine miles further on, I approach the tiny community of Glenelg (Earth), which is twinned with Glenelg on Mars! I stop outside the silent village hall noticing there's a public convenience that I don't hesitate to use. Just outside the village, the road leads me down a steep hill to a picturesque community-owned vehicle ferry service, which runs across the powerful currents of the narrows to Kylerhea on Skye.

Unbelievably, this is the original ferry crossing to the Isle of Skye, and it's not any old boat! Running every twenty minutes from April through to October and without the need to book, this is the last hand-operated turntable ferry in operation anywhere in the world. It simply means you drive on, and the boat's platform swivels round when it docks, meaning you just drive off! Besides a couple of vans with a handful of Americans enthusiastically taking photographs and waiting for their other friends to disembark, there's nobody else besides me and Bernie wanting to cross back over!

The little six-car ferry arrives and ties up alongside the slipway, a man jumps on board and manually turns the deck around, which is built on a turntable to allow the four smiling and enthusiastic passengers to disembark. I'm then ushered forward and slowly drive up the ramp onto the little red and green vessel. As the only passenger, I step out of the van onto the old wooden planked deck and lean curiously over the rails to look out to the cloud covered hills of Skye and the dark black waters. Although it only takes five minutes to cross, I notice seals swimming in the water, and a friendly conversation ensues with Colin, the Ferry Master: "Good morning to you! Are you needing a return? No? Alright, that'll be £15. But don't worry! If you want to come back this way, I'll recognise you and I'll only charge you for the return, which is £25, so you'll owe me just a tenner!"

Colin swivels the deck around when we arrive on the opposite banks and waves me cheerily goodbye as I bump down the ramp. Quite appropriately, the Isle of Skye takes its name from the old Norse *sky-a*, meaning "Cloud Island," which is a Viking reference to the often mist-enshrouded hillsides. And today is no exception! It's the second largest of Scotland's islands, after Lewis and Harris, extending fifty miles long, and over the next day I'm hoping to take in its raw beauty here in the Inner Hebrides.

The little one-lane track turns up and over the browning, bracken clad hillsides until it reaches the A87 intersection on the southern part of the island. Heading westwards, I'm beginning to see it's surprisingly a fairly busy road, with many more speeding cars and vans than I'd expected. But hopefully, looking down at my map, the place I'd chosen would again be "far from the madding crowds." I drive through Broadford, which—with its twenty-four hour petrol station, cash machine, and supermarket—is an essential service centre for the scattered communities in southern Skye. The road continues to hug the eastern shores until passing a few lochs, I turn off at Drynoch to a tiny road and head westwards through forested slopes and along the foot of the spectacular Cullin Hills, which in size look more like mountains!

The road ends at Glenbrittle Campsite, looking out to wild and misty Loch Brittle Beach. The van's parked up next to a massive, green corrugated building with its own red telephone box, and I'm greeted inside by a trendy wood panelled deli and café, which at some point *The Daily Telegraph* had voted as the UK's Number One Campsite! Even now, there are more than a handful of people, but I'm told I can park up anywhere there's space, and there's quite a lot. The van's driven close to the water's edge, but due to the rain and grass-sodden terrain, I wisely choose a safer site on gravel. I certainly don't want to be asking for people to push me out of the mud tomorrow morning!

Although the seemingly colder weather doesn't look like it's going to improve much, the walking boots are enthusiastically put on, and I wander down to the seaweed strewn black sand on the edge of the receding shoreline. Bizarrely, on this expanse of beach, fine crystal white sand covers this dark, almost black, sand. I kneel down and with a stick inscribe into the white sand the words *Carpe Diem*, which turns black from the sand below. With the increasing wind and splattering of rain, a decision is needed on what to do next. The place is beautiful and would probably be even better if the sun was shining and less chilly, but with the next few days of ominous weather predictions, I'm not feeling too convinced I want to stay much longer. And that feeling makes me just want to start my journey back.

So, sitting back in Bernie and keeping myself reasonably warm with a brew and a hot water bottle on my lap, I make plans to drive around the Isle of Skye tomorrow to see as much as possible before then driving as far south as possible to cover the miles homebound!

As forecast, the next morning is identical to the last one, with soft, cold drizzling rain and not much of a view as I look out through the curtains from my cosy little bed. Without a second thought, that's me decided. Leaving the campsite, I start my clockwise drive around Skye. It's not easy to get lost here, as there's pretty much only one road—but what views! An hour later through the mountainous, grassy wild terrain, the sun is desperately trying to peek through the drab clouds but without much success. And so, after about another hour's casual drive, it's with dark, dismal skies that I take a small diversion to entertain myself and come to Skye's most famous historic building, the popular Dunvegan Castle of the MacLeod Clan. Timing is perfect, as it's just about to open, and so I eagerly jog up to the front desk to avoid queuing behind the bus load that has also just arrived! Set on the quiet waterside, the location is spectacular, and a group of us enter the fortress-like studded entrance door. Besides the usual castle stuff, like swords, silver, family portraits, and rugs strewn over the floors, there's a pretty spooky dungeon and then a beautiful walk that leads down to the water's edge, where you can jump onto a boat to go seal watching. I opt for the view instead and, stuffed with castle and sword-fighting facts, head back to the van.

Continuing northwards and up onto the A850, I'm surprised to see so many clusters of campsites and feel that this place in the summertime must be heaving. But isolation soon appears again as I head further north into the Trotternish Peninsula to view The Quiraing. Rather than drive all around the coast on the A855, I'd been strongly advised to cut through at Uig on the small unclassified mountain road, which would reveal the full splendour much more dramatically. The small, challenging road is exceptional in its beauty and the heights it comes to in revealing the mystical emerald green lands of The Quiraing. The place, so high up, is simply phenomenal, with contorted pillars and buttresses of eroded lava stretching far up into the sky. The "Pillar," the "Needle," and the "Prison" give that feeling of natural majesty, along with a feeling of mystery and antiquity in this hidden place. There's even a car park to take a closer look before the scarily, dramatic descent back down to the coast.

Heading southwards along the dangerous looking steep cliffside road, the whole place is shrouded by bizarre looking stony shapes. But nothing beats what I see next. The Old Man of Storr is a spectacular pillar of stone, the highest on this Trotternish Peninsula, and clearly visible from the road. This extraordinary sight is the one you probably most associate with the Isle of Skye and probably features the most on postcards.

The Isle of Skye has certainly given me my dose of adrenalin, and it's not long before I'm driving over the bridge and pointing Bernie southwards onto the A87 towards Fort William and shortly back onto the familiar A82. I'd anticipated that, with the revised long drive today, returning southwards and covering almost three hundred miles, I'd need to keep a close lookout for somewhere to stay later on, as nothing had been booked. So, towards the end of the afternoon, approaching Loch Lomond, I'm getting desperate to find a quiet campsite or basically anywhere I can safely park up for the night.

Paul Theroux, another Aries solo intrepid traveller like me, says in one of his books, "I'm not by nature a networker or a looker-up of people, so I am always dependent on chance meetings, on dumb luck, on the kindness of strangers." That's also me to a T, and at this stage in the trip, I am also needing a bit of dumb luck to find a place to park the van up at such short unplanned notice.

But that seemingly simple need couldn't have been more difficult. Everywhere along Loch Lomond, the shore seems to be lined with either chalets, hotels, or private "members only" campsites. At each one I stop at, even with a pleading face, I'm told to get on my way!

It's not until I reach almost the tip of the loch, close to Alexandria, and with the daylight quickly fading that I only by chance curiously catch sight of a small row of campervans parked up next to each other in a quiet little road, hidden by trees. My indicator quickly flashes, and driving down the lane, I find a perfect spot on the roadside, between two vans and next to an old stone wall, with uninterrupted views out onto Loch Lomond. The clouds have now all but disappeared, and there's a beautiful blue and purple tone to the clear darkening sky that gradually turns a warm pinky-orange out onto the horizon. This is my first taste of "wild camping," and although it feels slightly naughty, it also feels good simply sitting in my little foldable chair on the pavement, looking out to the peaceful waters and unexpected beautiful sunset.

It's only the next morning that I realize "wild-campers" don't hang around much, and by the time I've sorted myself out to leave with the rising sun, most of the other vans are following suit or have already left. In fact, I'd gotten up so early that by the time I'm driving around misty Glasgow on the M8, I overtake a van driver diligently brushing his teeth! I decide to extend the trip just slightly by making just one more stop-off before arriving in Hereford the next day. As it is on my way, I decide to cut the trip in half and stop in the Lake District, which was another place I hadn't set foot in for a long time.

Just above Derwent Water and Keswick, I drive through a little country lane no wider than four sheep and find the working Lane Farm in Thornthwaite with a pleasant campsite in their surrounding fields. I'm in luck. The location is beautiful, particularly on this day, the World Environmental Day, with summer sunshine and bright blue cloudless skies. It feels like another world from yesterday's dark, grey drizzling skies up in the Isle of Skye.

For one last time, I pull on my walking boots and strike out to the neighbouring and picturesque village of Braithwaite to sit outside the historic Coledale Inn with a cold refreshing shandy to soak up the mesmerizing and calming views across the green hill-lined valley. I'm thoroughly content and feel the whole journey through some of the most isolated parts of Scotland was something I would definitely be tempted to do again. The entire trip, which started in London, up through Northumberland, around Scotland, and back down through the Lake District to the Welsh Borders, has pretty much taken me around most of our beautiful and cherished Great Britain.

Finishing my drink, I wander back down through the lanes to the campsite. But what should be a wild cacophony of chirping wild birds and bleating sheep, is sadly overshadowed with the distant rumbling of traffic and impatient drivers speeding through the popular valley below. Not to worry. I'll be back on the road tomorrow with Bernie and hopefully heading to a slightly more peaceful place somewhere on the Welsh Borders.

PART FOUR

EIRE—WITH ALL THE LUCK OF THE IRISH!

Although Ireland is only about fifty miles across the Irish Sea from Wales, it was never a place I had ever been wildly tempted to visit, except for that quick one-day business trip to Dublin many moons ago. So embarrassingly, my affinity and knowledge of the place wasn't too strong. But I had heard that it had endured hard times with the disastrous potato famines of the mid-1850s during which almost a million people died, forcing many others to emigrate to different parts of the world from a hop over the Irish Sea to Liverpool to all the way across the Atlantic to Boston, Massachusetts. But I associated and visualized it far more for its lush green fields covered with lucky four-leaf clovers and hence the name Emerald Isle, it's worldwide fame for its black frothy Guinness beer, the rambling colourful horse-drawn gypsy caravans, the little bearded leprechaun fairies sometimes appearing to play their mischief, and a country famous and proud of their fine thoroughbred horses and racing.

My only other link with Ireland was finding two old dusty, out of focus, black and white photographs of my parents, who had spent their honeymoon in County Cork during the fifties. One image shows them sitting uncomfortably and somewhat nervously on two large draught horses, while the other photo has my father upside down planting his lips onto and kissing the Blarney Stone!

But during the spring and summer months of 2009 my ties with Ireland would mysteriously become incredibly strong and for all the wrong, and right, reasons! It was the first weekend of May, and I was up in Hereford visiting my mother and trying to get my head together on the fact that my long-term relationship with my partner was slowly falling away and that I wasn't happy. I felt like I wanted some crazy light relief.

Looking over the newspaper, my mother smiles and points at the back pages. "I know it's not the Grand National, but why don't we do a flutter on the 2000 Guineas in Newmarket tomorrow?"

She digs into her purse. "Here's a couple of quid. Go on over the road to the bookies and see what you think looks good to win!"

Without anything else to do, I take the newspaper and look down at the names of the horses to see which one grabs my attention. With no knowledge whatsoever of the flat racing scene I have absolutely no clues. But one name stares up at me. and although he's not the favourite to win at eight to one, I like the quirky name of the Irish colt "Sea the Stars." That's what I'm also needing at this moment in time, to see beyond my current life's situation. The next day, Sea the Stars very unexpectedly but clearly wins the big race, and we happily share the £18 winnings, which feels like an easily won fortune!

From that day on, something bizarrely takes over my

common sense, and I become increasingly obsessed with this little bay horse and where it's going on to race next. The following month in June it's The Epsom Derby, also famous for those lipsticked ladies and their giant theatrical hats, and I gamble an increasingly ambitious £50 bet on the bay to win. He does just that, and I'm immediately almost £200 richer!

By now, "Sea The Stars" is making news, not just in the *Racing Post*, but in the nationwide press, and I also start to learn about the intriguing world of ante-post betting! It's simply a bet placed months before the horse racing course's betting market has opened. It's made on the expectation that the price of the horse is currently more favourable than it will be when the market opens closer to the race. Although a bigger risk, this was the only way to potentially make bigger bucks before each of his races, when on the day the odds and winnings for a horse like this would become almost worthless.

For what sounds crazy now, by mid-June I take a massive leap of faith and spend almost all my £2000 hard-earned savings on a massively risky ante-post bet. I bet for this one horse, to win all his races throughout the entire season up until October! Something almost unheard of. For each of his races I continue gambling, with subsequent wins now coming in at the July Eclipse Stakes in Sandown, the York Juddmonte International Stakes in August, and the Irish Champion Stakes in Leopardstown, Ireland, in September. The regular betting shops and online sites are getting to know me, and so without joking, I have to go to different establishments further afield or on the other side of town to place additional bets on the same horse and the same races. That summer the whole of Ireland is on a crazy high watching the impossible happen, and I am literally on a once in a lifetime winning streak, never for once thinking I'd lose. "Sea the Stars" finally wins his last ever historic race at the Prix de l'Arc de Triomphe in Paris on the 4 October, on which I'd gambled another four figure sum.

That next day, discreetly leaving my office at lunchtime to visit the betting shop and collect the winnings on the Paris race and all the ante-post betting I'd done throughout the season, the William Hill clerk behind the counter looks at the collection of tickets in disbelief. He apologizes but tells me I'll need to come back a lot later, as they just don't have enough cash in their safes! I make, in my estimations, a substantial amount of money to help with my unknown future. For a few months afterwards, I am still tempted and continue with other horses racing at the end of season's US Breeders Cup in Kentucky and the Melbourne Cup in Australia. But the adrenalin isn't the same, and besides minuscule wins, I am now also dangerously losing on my bets. I know only too well, that it is time to stop being tempted and walk away from what I'd jumped into at the start of the year. I can understand only too well how easy it is for others to fall into a gambling addiction, believing there is always another impossible win.

"Sea the Stars," regarded by many as one of the greatest racehorses of all time, is now retired back in Ireland at the Aga Khan's Gilltown Stud in County Kildare. This one miraculous and never before seen racing season, with the absurd and incalculable risks I'd taken, gives me the strength and positivity to move forward with my life knowing that anything is possible.

OUR WILD ATLANTIC WAY

TWO GIRLS AND TWO BIKES ON A MOTORCYCLING TRIP AROUND THE EMERALD ISLE

Riding leisurely up and over those rolling Welsh hillsides on that sunny Spring day in May, the pretty Pembrokeshire coastal town of Goodwick, and twin town of neighbouring Fishguard, comes into view with its ferry port and docks. A sensible plan had been made to meet Olly close to the port to fill up with petrol, grab a drink, and get ourselves sorted before boarding the Stena Line ship.

To be totally truthful, this is pretty much the very first time I'd organized and agreed to travel by motorcycle for an extended period with somebody else, and I simply have no idea on what to expect or how we'll cope together for an entire two weeks! Most of my biking travels, either in Britain or further afield, had always been done on my own. That's when I felt the most freedom; to come and go as I pleased, without any major discussion and planning things accordingly. But this opportunity is too good to miss. Olly is a fellow positive, outgoing friend who also just happens to like motorcycles, travel, good food, and with her ever smiling face, had a light hearted approach to life. So, I guess, the perfect travelling buddy.

I pull up into the retro Beaches Diner forecourt and look around. Parked up on its own is a spanking new black Triumph Street Twin 900cc with two matching black hard-cased travel panniers. Smiling in recognition, I park up beside the shiny bike, knowing that Olly had already arrived.

Looking at both bikes, the difference couldn't be more apparent—beautiful tradition with strange eccentricity. My newly built and customized Honda Rebel Bobber, with its glittering gold paint job, the silver wings representing freedom painted on the tank, the black heart-shaped sissy bar representing passion, the leather tasselled saddle bags and its handcrafted inscribed "Carpe Diem" leather brown seat, had recently replaced my original 790cc Triumph Bonneville. This new bike, with its thick big rubber tyres and strong looking but much lighter and lower frame, looked a lot more powerful than its 500cc engine. But for me, and the reasons I finally said goodbye to my Bonnie, was that the Rebel really was a lot lower, so I could finally place my feet safely on the ground and was a weight that I could ultimately have greater ease in lifting up should it fall over or in simply just manoeuvring it around in confined or difficult areas. Although I'd only clocked up a couple of thousand miles, I am already very happy with my decision.

As I enter the diner, with its plush red leather banquettes, Olly, with a matching red lipstick smile, stands up and walks over from her map-covered table.

Both hugging each other, Olly's the first to utter a few excited words in her lovely soft Welsh accent, "Oh my goodness. We're actually here! My trip from Aberystwyth along the coast was fine. A few rainy drizzles but that soon disappeared. How was yours from Hereford?"

Walking back to the table after ordering mugs of coffee, I place my helmet next to her map and smile back. "No problem whatsoever. But it started pelting down halfway at Llandovery. where I had no choice but to stop for a brew and some warmth at the bikers West End Cafe. It was freezing cold, and my gloves got drenched through. But you can bet that I'm pretty excited that we'll be getting onto the ship in only an hour or so, and then by mid-afternoon we'll be in Ireland!"

Sitting opposite us is an old guy casually and contentedly reading a local newspaper and, from time to time, looking at his watch. He looks up, nods courteously to us, and with a strong Welsh accent introduces himself, "I couldn't help but overhear what you were both talking about. I'm here to pick up my daughter and grandchildren from the boat, which will be arriving soon. If it's your first time over to Ireland by sea, you won't be able to imagine what it used to be like."

We both sit forward in our seats and look over with curious encouraging nods to hear more. And with that, Evan is transported to another time and, with half closed eyes, searches for his memories: "No wonder my Welsh name means 'Little Warrior.' It was exciting back then exploring. We were just nineteen years old back then in 1955 when us kids would jump onto the cattle truck ship from Ellesmere to Dublin. That was the only way to get over to Ireland back then, over sixty years ago. When we got there, the trucks went to the Dublin Cattle Market located on Prussia Street and nicknamed 'Cowtown.' It was back then that we reckon it was the largest weekly livestock sale in Europe. Me and my mates would walk into the pubs, which were open from 7AM, and there we'd see seventy to eighty glasses already lined up along the bar, as it took about an hour and a half for the Guinness Porter beer to settle!" He chuckles, stands up and waves us goodbye.

And with that, we also get up to leave, jump on our bikes, with Olly looking in the mirror to add just a little extra red lippie, and slowly ride over to the port. It's there we're directed to go to the front of the line, passing all the other vehicles, and wait with just four other bikers. The large ship has already docked, and lines of cars and caravans are slowly bumping down the ramps and spewing out of its mouth. The turnaround to get the ship back out again is surprisingly quick. I smile reassuringly to Olly and put my thumbs up, as a uniformed guy waves the two of us forward, to ride into the ship. Inside its belly, further hands wave and direct us to a wall near the ship's bow exit, then the deckhands quickly and professionally tie the bikes securely down. Taking our helmets and valuables, we climb three steep flights of stairs to the lounge area, and first onto the ship, we wisely grab and crash into two armchairs looking directly out to sea. Boots and jackets are taken off and we stretch out in pure decadence.

For the next three and a quarter hours the Stena Line sails briskly over the relatively calm expanse of The Irish Sea, with only a few other boats within eyesight bobbing out and disappearing into the horizon. The day is clear and the sky a cloudless palette of watery blue.

Olly is still looking down attentively at the map, no doubt strategizing on how we're going to find the first place we'd booked to stay at tonight. "So if I'm right, leaving Rosslare we simply need to keep on the N25 westbound towards Waterford until we get to Rosbercon, then take the minor road R704 to Mullinavat in County Kilkenny. It's probably no more than forty-odd miles so shouldn't take us more than an hour. That's if we don't get lost!"

I nod, "Sounds right to me. Brid, the farmer's wife at Glenraha Farm, said it was just up a lane from there to Ballinaraha. I'm quite excited, as she said if we arrive early enough, we can even help her husband milk the cows in their parlour!"

The idea of staying in different and eclectic places was a priority for us from the outset. We'd definitely decided not to camp, using the totally acceptable excuse to us, that it was extra luggage and weight on the bikes! But deep down, we just didn't want to get soaking wet and found it hard to be without those little luxuries, like a nice warm shower in the evenings, a welcoming drink and meal, as well as comfortable beds with fresh linen to sleep in. But instead of staying in the normal B&Bs or hotels, we'd decided to do just that little extra bit of research and find some "out there" places. Tonight, was no exception, and thanks to the Irish Farmers Directory, we'd be staying at a working Irish dairy farm in the verdant low range Booley Hills of Kilkenny.

The ferry finally arrives into Rosslare Harbour, which already looks like a pretty isolated place. Announcements are made that we can return to our vehicles. We smile excitedly and run quickly down to the lower deck, untying the bikes, nervously putting our helmets on, and starting up in anticipation. We're waved on and carefully ride down the ramp and bump back onto terra firma. The smiling Customs Officer simply asks us where we're going, interested to know our nationalities, and doesn't even request any ID! Directions out onto the N25 are simple, passing the obligatory Aldi and Lidl. For the majority of the journey, Olly takes the lead through the quiet countryside roads, past thatched cottages, and riding a perfect, leisurely fifty-five to sixty miles per hour. As predicted, and within an hour, we're approaching green fields full of black and white Friesian cattle.

Timing couldn't be better, as the cows have already been collected from their pastures and are patiently lining up, waiting their turn to walk into the milking parlour. Half an hour later we're attired in borrowed wellington boots and rubber gloves, treading through the slurry, as red-cheeked Jim, dressed in green overalls and a woolly ski hat, enthusiastically leads us to the deafening sound of the mooing cows.

With his soft, sing-songy Irish accent Jim points over smiling, "So girls, would you like to have a go? Come and stand behind the cows. You can have four each! Take the cloth and clean her udder and teats. Then like this, attach the suction device onto each teat, and there you'll see the milk automatically flowing into the receiving container. We sell it for just thirty-two cents a litre, and this milk is turned into dry baby formula milk. It's exported to China and third world countries. We normally produce more than 2,400 litres a day from all our cows! It's perfect here for the cows. We have rich, green fields, and it's not cold in the winter, but it is wet!"

I'm totally surprised by what he's just told us and where the milk ends up on the other side of the world. I look at Olly trying her hardest to get the contraptions attached, and I can't help but start laughing as I also endeavour to be as gentle as possible without being kicked. Jim seems pleased with our tom-foolery and mentions proudly that we'll be drinking some of that same fresh raw milk tomorrow morning at breakfast!

It all feels like it's been a long day with so much that has already happened. Back inside the farmhouse and flicking through today's free weekly *The Kilkenny Reporter*, we find a place nearby to eat. After a lift down to The Rising Sun in Mullinavat. we find ourselves in an old barn that was apparently a place Cromwell's horses stayed during those turbulent times. After a hearty supper of local pork, turnip, and our first of many feasts of potatoes, then drank down with our first Guinness and Smithwicks, the farm beckons us back for a deep, deep sleep.

I'm pleasantly woken to the gentle humming in the other bed of a very familiar song that my father used to sing to us as children when we were travelling in his van. I smile, due to its significance, and join in until we're both singing some of the lyrics and jumping about getting ready to leave on this sunny day—

It's a long way to Tipperary,
It's a long way to go.
It's a long way to Tipperary
To the sweetest girl I know!

Up to mighty London came
An Irish man one day,
All the streets were paved with gold,
So everyone was gay!
Singing songs of Piccadilly,
Strand and Leicester Square,
'Til Paddy got excited and
And he shouted to them there:
It's a long way to Tipperary,
It's a long way to go.
It's a long way to Tipperary
To the sweetest girl I know!

A generous Irish breakfast of bacon, sausages, baked beans, eggs, mushrooms, and some bubble and squeak are served up, and I take a sip of tea smiling, "I can't believe you also know that tune and that Tipperary will be one of our first ports of call this morning!"

Olly smiles, "Yes, I thought we'd get ourselves into the mood!"

Bags are packed and tied down onto the bikes. Farewells are said, but not before Brid excitedly rushes out, hands me a wooden Irish hockey stick, and bashes a stone-hard ball my way to hit it back to her in the courtyard!

She smiles at my skills, "May the luck of the Irish lead you to the happiest heights and the highway you travel be lined with green lights!"

We wave gratefully goodbye to the kind, smiling farmers as we trundle down the empty lanes. We're off to a good start in partnering up for this trip, as we both whole-heartedly agree that an early start will be best so we can leisurely cover the miles and not have to arrive late, fiddling with maps when it gets dark. At this stage, we'd both unanimously decided not to use any sat-nav and instead endeavour to find our way using the old-fashioned way of navigation with just maps and simply asking people the way. And I'm starting to see that so far, Ireland seems to be a lot less busy than where we'd originally come from yesterday and that life somehow seems to be a lot slower. But today we'd agreed to undertake the longest trip we'd do on any one day, in order to get as quickly as possible to the west coast and properly start our journey along the famous Wild Atlantic Way. Although not massive mileage, we'd reckoned today would be about 150 miles riding gradually north-east through the centre of the country until arriving at our destination of the arty, bohemian city of Galway, where we'd spend a couple of nights.

Hours of strategic discussions had pursued long before the trip in which roads to take, ideally the smaller the better, and would we have the time or energy to make a fairly significant detour to see the Cliffs of Moher, west of Limerick. The decision was we'd decide as we rode and without any pressure see how we felt, but at least felt reassured we had a firm destination to get to and beds booked to sleep in.

After a fairly short burst southwards on the M9, we turn westwards at the busy port of Waterford, Ireland's oldest city, dating back over 1,100 years to Viking times and famous now as the home of Waterford crystal, onto the N24 crossing the country. Before long, we enter into landlocked County Tipperary, with its fertile fields and apple trees full of spring's pink and white blossoms. Along this remote road and riding through Clonmel, I smile when I see a sign with a familiar name. It's here that Bulmers, established from my hometown of Hereford, have one of their factories making Magners apple cider. I'm more than happy to simply follow Olly as we continue sweeping through the small town of Cahir and, before long, enter Tipperary for our obligatory "tea-break" stop. In our estimations, this is probably a third of the way and so almost sixty miles already under our belts.

Walking away from the bikes in one of the town's anonymous car parks, the smiling face of an "Irish Mammy" approaches us with her flowered shopping trolley. Clad in an oversize grey rain coat, with her apron still on underneath it and rollers under her knitted hat, she warmly smiles at us, "Oh, I am impressed with you two girls! You're both divils with those big machines! Make sure to wrap up or you'll get a chill in your kidneys!"

She then says something indecipherable like, "Giorraíonn beirt bother!" And continues, "Don't worry it's only an old Gaelic expression that means 'two people shorten a road,' like you're doing. We Irish people are deeply communal, and if a trip is necessary, be it long or short, it's always preferable to have companionship. So, you're doing the right thing. May God be with you. Go Girls!"

We both smile gently at her from hearing the first of many warm, unprompted welcomes we're to receive travelling across Ireland. "Tipp town," as it's locally known, is itself a bit sad and run-down, with no real sights except a sculpture we see commemorating the song we'd just sung earlier and a pretty decent coffee at the French Quarter Café in the Tipperary Arts Centre. Replenished, we set off back onto the N24 entering County Limerick, again crossing low-lying farmland, surrounded by uplands and ever-visible mountains. With no real thirst to enter the boisterously urban setting of Limerick, in contrast to the countryside we were riding through, we cross its tidal reaches of Ireland's longest river, the Shannon, and continue heading westwards where it joins the Shannon Estuary on the N18. Ireland's third largest airport, Shannon, comes and goes but, in the old days, it was a vital fuelling stop for piston-engine planes lacking the range to make it between the mainlands of North America and Europe.

We've still a way to go, and although it would be simple to just jump onto the M18 motorway all the way to Galway, we decide that was definitely not what we've set out to do or what we wanted to do. We'd be missing so much on the start of our coastal wanderings. So, after a few miles northbound, we get off the main road as soon as possible and head towards Ennis to find a place to stop to browse the maps and find the smallest possible roads that will lead us up and along out to the coast.

Ennis is a pleasant enough little hub, and it's here we stop to fill up with petrol and stretch our legs. The panniers are also filled with freshly baked Irish soda bread, Irish cheddar cheese, sweet tomatoes, obligatory chocolate bars to sustain our energy, and a couple of bottles of water; and all this with the intention to then find an attractive and interesting place to stop for lunch. Starting the bikes up again, the main street leads us past the thirteenth century Ennis Friary and out onto the N85.

At Fountain Cross, Olly's indicator once again starts flashing, this time turning right and onto the pleasant, tiny R476 country northbound road to Corofin. We're finally on what I can only describe as the most beautiful, quiet, peaceful, and lost lane, which leads us across green patchwork fields and deeper into this unknown countryside. We swiftly pass the tiny quaint village of Corofin on the River Fergus, located next to pretty little lakes with tiny rowing boats moored up on their grassy banks. Then it's past the tiny settlement of no more than three homes of Kilnaboy, where we pass an old roofless church and its graveyard. The whole place is now starting to get a wilder feel as the roads start to climb a little higher and the fields become larger, ultimately losing their fences to create simply open pasture and moorland.

For the first time, we stop on the side of the road and simply turn off and silence our bikes to quietly look over the calm countryside, feeling the warm breeze coming over to gently stroke our senses. The stress levels, if ever there had been any since we left our respective homes, seem to be magically disappearing into this half-earthly half-heavenly place. We both knowingly smile to each other and get back onto the bikes with a spring in our steps.

It's just past the junction heading up along the R480 that again we stop to see the ghostly, ruined, five storey Leamaneh Castle, dating back to the fifteenth century. It's a rare example of fifteenth to seventeenth century transitional architecture from a castle to fortified country house. Unlike many of the castles in Ireland, this one is unmaintained and, due to its poor state of repair, was not accessible for closer inspection on the privately owned farming land surrounded by robust dry stone walls. Most of the stone walls we'd be travelling past in western Ireland were constructed in the last two hundred years to form field divisions and clear the ground. They were cleverly built without mortar and hence the name *dry stone* walls, with similar walls seen in the Cotswolds in England, Wales, and Scotland.

Leaving the rich fertile fields, we climb up into the mountains and onto dry, stony heather moorland. It's then, reaching the top of the hilly road and coming to a flat area with views that stretch out for miles and miles all around us, that we feel we've found the perfect place for our first outdoor picnic. It's also home to a beautiful old roofless church and cemetery with unbelievably, as we discover, some of the crosses and tombstones actually residing within the old crumbling church. Sitting here all on our own and wiggling our bare feet through the grass, munching our simple Irish soda bread sandwiches, and only hearing the wind and distant sheep gives us a euphoric sense of freedom.

That freedom continues as the road becomes ever wilder, stretching across the curious Burren Country. It feels like a lonely, pumice-stone moon-land of bubbling, solidified vast grey rock—in layers, folds, crevices, cracks, and fissures from the mountains down to the hidden sea but decorated with greenery, heather expanses, hidden rare flowers, and white spring blossoms. The sky is blue, and thick white cumulus clouds lick the horizon, enticing us to travel further.

Slightly further up this road we're met by the small N67 and cross over to the A477, which now heads north, beautifully hugging the coast all the way to Galway. Or we could have turned left to venture further southwards to see the Cliffs of Moher, but time is racing by, and with clouds gathering, we decide to begin riding our first leg of the Wild Atlantic Way northwards.

The Wild Atlantic Way, Ireland's western coastline hugging the Atlantic, is one of the world's most stunning and longest coastal routes in the world, covering 1,600 miles (2,600 km) in length. Its stunning stretches of jagged cliffs, snow white sand beaches, and tapestry-patterned fields winds its way all along the coastline from the Inishowen Peninsula in the north all the way down to the picturesque town of Kinsale, County Cork, in the south. It's spread over nine counties: County Donegal, Leitrim, Sligo, Mayo, Galway, Clare, Kerry, and Cork.

Our chosen route will cover three of these Counties: Clare, Galway, and incorporating Connemara and Mayo with its beautiful less-visited northern islands.

It's here we start to see the sand hills and beaches of Fanore as we head around to Black Head, where the deep Atlantic comes alongside us like a ship. The small stone harbour of Kinvara sits at the south-eastern corner of Galway Bay and overlooks the little island with the Castle of Dunguaire. Filled with vividly painted old buildings, this charming village is our next pit stop for a drink at the welcoming Pier Head Bar overlooking the calm bay waters with boats and their massive hulls pulled out of the water and propped up like stranded whales. The view is fairly clear, and we incredibly get a glimpse of the three Aran Islands, only six miles off shore again like whales barely showing their curved backs and fins over the water.

With just twenty miles left to navigate along the N67 Wild Atlantic Way to Galway, we both reckon we've got it all easily sorted as we ride along grey stone-walled roads overlooking green fields and wind around the little inlets. But not quite! Within minutes, the skies unexpectedly cover over, and arriving just on the outskirts of Galway, the rain starts to seriously pelt down. We have no other choice but to both indicate to stop on the side of the road and run for shelter under large roadside trees while quickly pulling our waterproof trousers back on again. The only consolation to this interruption is having a spontaneous chat with a fellow traveller, also standing under the trees. Tom is a retired seventy-three year old, attired in a skin hugging cycling suit and holding a sleek looking road racing bicycle. He's already cycled thirty miles and was just a few miles from home. He wishes us well as he bravely steps out and continues peddling down the rain sodden road.

I turn to face Olly, "So are you ready for your next adventure in staying somewhere different from last night? Tonight, we're going to experience staying at a hostel! Not any old hostel, but one of the best Galway has to offer and in the middle of town where all the action is. We need to find and get close to the docklands, where it is."

Olly smiles and with tongue in cheek replies, "Yes, believe it or not, I've never stayed at a hostel, so it'll be interesting sleeping in bunkbeds and sharing the room with total strangers. Can't wait!"

Riding through the one-way system in Galway to find our hostel doesn't turn out to be that easy, but we finally find the little road and park up to unload the bikes. After checking in and leaving our stuff on our bunkbeds, and with no parking at the hostel, our next job is to find a place to park our bikes. With its one-way systems and busy roads, it takes us more than a while to find the safe, enclosed multi-storey car park where we'll be leaving our precious bikes for the next day or so. With chains linked between both front wheels and covers placed safely over the bikes, we thirstily go looking for a place serving beers. Just below our Galway City Hostel is the thumping Darcy's Bar, with live Irish music already playing as we wander in! We grab two Galway Hookers and sit down to nourish ourselves with this strong Irish Stout. Obvious jokes aside, Galway hookers are actually the iconic small sailing boats that were very much essential for local seafaring up to the twentieth century. Small, tough, and highly manoeuvrable, these wooden boats are undergoing a positive resurgence, thanks to weekend leisure sailors. The hulls are jet back, due to the pitch used for waterproofing, while the sails flying from the single mast are the distinctive red rust colour. We'd already seen sightings of them coming up along the Galway coast, but we were to see a lot more the further north we went.

Seated on two high stools, we stare at the stage tapping our feet. "So how many miles did we finally do, do you reckon, Olly?"

Olly pulls her glasses up onto her head and looks seriously down at her phone and to her tracker app, which should be fairly accurate. Her look is one of disbelief, and she scratches her head. She bursts out uncontrollably laughing, "This is hilarious! I think I cocked up with the tracker, which I set up at Tipperary to go to Galway. But I forgot to turn it off each time we stopped so the ninety-seven mile trip apparently took us seven and a half hours, with an average speed of thirteen miels per hour, because we stopped for lunch and I forgot to turn it off at the cemetery! Otherwise, we did a maximum speed of fifty-eight miles per hour. Come and have a look at this screenshot of us arriving and riding around Galway, getting lost and trying to find the parking. It's even worse."

And true to her word, the lines showing how many times we'd ridden around the same one-way system and up and down dead-end streets looks like a bowl of spaghetti! As for food that evening it certainly isn't pasta but a treat at McDonagh's in Quay Street, where we spoil ourselves with delicious local seared scallops and Galway Bay Stout. Tip-toeing lightly into our dorm later that night, with torches in hands, we giggle uncontrollably at trying to keep quiet and pray that the other girls won't return the favour by keeping us awake with their snoring.

Still giggling, I dig into my bag. "Try this as a new experience," as I offer her a pair of earplugs!

Next morning, there's no need to frantically grab things and start packing again, as we'd be putting our walking shoes on instead. But before all that I wanted to give Olly the total hostel experience and have breakfast in the communal area.

A noisy, excited buzz comes from the room as people are seated on stools around a communal table eating, chatting, and organizing their day. With what most are wearing, shorts and hoodies, it looks like a crowd of them are getting ready to leave for the hostel's organized surf trip out along the Wild Atlantic Way.

From the outset, wandering out past Eyre Square and heading towards the medieval city walled Spanish Arch, we see it exudes the feeling of the most engaging place, with friendly buskers and musicians out on the streets and lively cafés already drumming up business. No wonder it's been named as one of Ireland's most welcoming places and had been designated the European Capital of Culture for 2020. Being a Saturday, we were also in luck, as it was the only day for the lively Galway Street Market with its mountains of fresh cheeses, vegetables, locally sourced giant oysters, mussels, and scallops that naturally meant Olly's eyes were popping out with the choice, and our backpacks got quickly filled with the farmers' delicious produce. Walking over one of the bridges and the River Corrib, we enter the bohemian West Side of the city where historic little "hole in the wall" pubs like The Dew Drop Inn and the Crane Bar would come alive at night with their traditional Irish musicians and informal ceilidh. Mingled in-between are little craft shops and indie eateries ,nineteen to the dozen. Thirsty for a brew, we enter the beautiful Kai Café, and sitting on their colourful chairs with the sun streaming in, we eat and relish without hesitation their most sublime naughty delicacies.

We were being blessed with the weather with the brightest of blue skies. Walking back and crossing over to Earl's Island, hearing the sound of music we curiously wander into the copper green domed Galway Cathedral. Amazingly, under its Romanesque arches, we're the only visitors to capture a beautiful Catholic wedding taking place, with the proud father walking his daughter down the aisle. Crossing the Salmon Weir Bridge, with the roaring waters below are a handful of hardy anglers with their thigh-high grey waders agilely casting out in the middle of this fast-flowing river. The salmon and sea trout fishing season is officially open since February, running until September, and as most fish pass through here during May and June, this was definitely now a time for these guys to try their luck.

Arriving on the other side of the weir, a large stone plinth is etched with thoughts from George Moore, the famous Irish novelist (1852-1933), entitled "Hail and Farewell":

> *A lovely day it was, the town*
> *lying under a white canopy of cloud,*
> *not a wind in all the air, but a*
> *line of houses sheer and dim along*
> *the river mingling with grey shadows;*
> *and on the other bank there*
> *were waste places difficult to account for,*
> *ruins showing dimly through the soft*
> *diffused light, like old castles, but Yeats said*
> *they were ruins of ancient mills, for*
> *Galway had once been a prosperous town.*
> *Maybe, my spirit answered,*
> *but less beautiful than she is to-day.*

Indeed, Galway is truly beautiful, and besides playing a bet that I couldn't dress up as a Leprechaun that I actually did accomplish late at night in the town centre by putting my face through a cardboard image of one, our precious remaining hours are spent in ambling in and out of pubs absorbing the atmosphere, listening to the music of the fiddles, flutes, banjo, pipes, and accordion while trying to judge the best local stouts.

The departure from the hostel and the snoring dorm mates is an early one, having safely collected the bikes from the multi-storey car park and carefully loaded them back up again. So early, in fact, that we decide to miss the hostel's Weetabix and toast on offer and decide there must be something much better to tempt us out on the road. It's a day to pull on the jacket and waterproofs, as the skies are cloud packed, and before we know it, we're soon out of Galway and away along the sea-hugging R336 road through the bright, breezy seaside resort of Salthill, with fine views over the lake-like Galway Bay. We continue past Barna and out alongside more grey stone walls with the sea on our left and intermittent views of the Aran Islands in the very far distance. Leaving Spiddal, we still haven't seen any cafés open yet, but I guess even with our enthusiasm it's not surprising, as it is a Sunday and not yet nine o'clock!

It's then that the first of many unexpected, spontaneous, and wonderful detours take place. I see Olly's red indicator suddenly flashing to turn left. We trundle down a small country lane to the discreet Connemara Airport. We turn the keys to turn our engines off, and Olly pulls her helmet off, "I hope you don't mind, but I thought this would be a good place for finding the "little room" and also see what this place is all about. We might even get a coffee."

And indeed, with its walls covered in historic black and white Irish countryside photographs from a bygone age, from the farmers herding sheep, to them cutting peat and old men ambling up the stony roads with their walking sticks, we're pleasantly surprised in what we find. It feels no more like a modernized big shed, but it's actually the essential hub for ferrying passengers to the Aran Islands. Continuing on, we come to a crossroads at Costelloe, and I gasp out in happiness in seeing for the very first time the rounded beauty of the Connemara Mountains gently rising out from the horizon. Experiencing Connemara was definitely one of the main reasons I'd wanted to do this trip. And it's here at this quiet intersection that the long-awaited breakfast finally calls out to us from a little unassuming café. We opt for the generous choice of a full Irish "Bricfeasta" with all the trimmings, including black and white pudding.

Noticing the matching happiness exuding from Olly's face and not quite sure whether it's the hearty breakfast or the freedom of the road, I also smile quizzically.

Her finger is tracing her more and more crinkled map now with the odd coffee stain. "Before heading out along the coast to our final destination today at Roundstone, why don't we make a few little detours and take the roads over the islands here to Carraroe and Lettermullen."

Time is generously on our side, we have nothing to rush for, and the big mileage in any one day had been taken care of in getting to Galway. Now we could take all the time to explore and go out of our way, which had always been the plan.

I nod enthusiastically, glad we're on the same easy-going wavelength, and as we take our bread-wiped plates to the counter, our smiles broaden further as the aproned lady chirpily chimes, "And top o' the mornin' to ya!"

Our first detour leads us down to the little village of Carraroe along lost country lanes and finally to a pretty rocky coast with tiny beaches of golden, coral sand.

Then coming back and further along the remote R374, we start to ride and enter a world truly out on its' own. Well past the holiday homes, we ride over strange, wild, rocky countryside, we pass over small narrow bridges with their flowing currents, see small round currachs hauled up onto the waterside, and just the odd white cottage dotted about for what must be a truly remote life. The vistas are becoming more and more deserted with the rocks . . . sea . . . bleakness . . . fine views over the mazed, island coasts . . . to mountains . . . beauty . . . quietness . . . along the road to the Islands . . . Bealadangan . . . Lettermore . . . Gorumna . . . Lettermullen.

Just as we're about to cross the final, tiny stone-walled bridge to the very tip of Golam Head, we're stopped in our tracks by the only traffic we've seen in quite a while. A large herd of white cattle and their calves are already ambling across the road, shepherded only by three small boys casually walking and prodding them from behind. With our engines politely turned off, they quietly pass between us and finally disappear further up the road through a gate. We also shortly turn around and head back through the flat stone bracken covered lowlands and over the wild narrow bridge roads, each one connecting the little islands to create this natural necklace of wonder.

Arriving back up at the café, we turn our bikes left and head this time westwards, returning onto the Wild Atlantic Way R340 road that continues to tightly hug this spectacular wild coastline, while we grab views every now and again of pretty little islands. The place feels so remote, with strange, rustic rocky land, until we reach Kilkieran, which provides unadulterated Bay-Island views of where we'd just come from. Without exaggeration, this place is quiet and seemingly off the radar of any other bikers or campers, which we'll gleefully accept. We then sweep up to Carna, a small settlement in Connemara in County Galway, for a stop at a petrol station noting a litre of unleaded is 1.45 euros, being slightly cheaper than back home in England. These remote petrol stations seem to serve a variety of purposes from their normal job of filling tanks to being a local supermarket, a hub of gossip and catching up on the latest news, a post office, and a place to buy tickets for the popular Irish National Lottery. The Irish Lotto, taking place every Wednesday and Saturday, regularly creates multi-millionaires, thanks to its favourable odds of winning the jackpot that's worth a minimum of two million euros and rises quickly, thanks to rollovers. Paying for the petrol, the attendant simply says, "Go raibh maith agat," and as I quizzically look back, he smiles and adds, "Thank you." Being in a strong Gaeltacht, or Irish-speaking region, up along this western coast, it's not surprising that most people here will only be speaking Irish back at home.

The same road clings up and around the coast, with our bikes purring contentedly, until we reach Cashel, with its little inlets and views of the jostling hills in the background. It's my indicator which lights up now as I come to a stop and can't resist walking up to my other idea of Ireland—lovely, little brown native Irish donkeys with their long pointy ears, dark spectacle rings around their eyes, grey muzzles, and shaggy coats. They docilely approach the fence and, probably thinking I have a carrot or two, stretch their heads out in greeting. Today, these three donkeys don't have much luck, besides receiving a gentle pat on their necks. But along with hedgehogs and red squirrels, they definitely fit into the category of "amiable animals."

Donkeys, especially in the west of the country, played a key role in rural lives, including clearing rocky fields, moving turf from bogs, ploughing, transport of people and goods, grinding corn, and finally, more nowadays for recreation and as family pets. The advent of motorised transport and tractors meant that donkeys have gradually become less important as working animals, but up until and for much of the twentieth century, parts of Ireland remained in relative poverty. A report of the Department of Agriculture in 1971—less than fifty years ago—stated that less than twenty-five per cent of households had toilets, eighteen per cent had bathrooms, seventy-five per cent had electricity, twenty-one per cent had television, three per cent had telephones, and twenty-six per cent had motorcars. It's very likely that many of these homes still depended on donkeys for some of the traditional tasks that needed done on farms.

Not far now from Roundstone, we continue following the bumpy, narrow road though deserted, flat bog land and rocky moorlands until we both notice brick-shaped mounds of black peat piled sky high. It's here both our indicators spontaneously light up, and we bring the bikes to a stop. It looks like all this peat has been recently harvested by hand, as blanket bogs can't be cut mechanically, and very soon, once they've dried out, they'll be taken away for fuel in the local cottages and farms. Some may even be taken to local petrol stations, where we've seen it being sold alongside the potatoes!

The road becomes ever flatter as we sweep around the water inlets with their sprinklings of white, thatched cottages, until Roundstone appears from across the wild Bertraghboy Bay. Clustered around a small boat-filled harbour with lobster trawlers and traditional currach boats, with tarred canvas bottoms stretched over their wicker frames, it's picture perfect and feels totally peaceful. Lobster pots have been hauled up and piled onto the harbour floors. And now with bright blue skies, it's the kind of Irish village we'd dreamed of finding. We ride up the empty main street, past colourful terraced houses and inviting pubs, to stop outside Island View B&B overlooking the beautiful silent bay. With today's mission accomplished, we have no other tasks to complete besides taking a good, long walk to work up a good appetite for this evening's gourmet delights. We're surrounded by some of the best fishing grounds on the west coast of Ireland. And so that evening at wonderful O'Dowds pub, we raise our glasses in toast, as bountiful seafood platters of Roundstone lobster, local crab claws, fresh and smoked salmon, mussels, baked and raw oysters, langoustines, and prawns—most of which are sourced off the old stone dock directly opposite us—are kindly brought to our table with the warmest of Irish hospitality.

Unbelievably, another sun-drenched morning almost touching a staggering twenty degrees, takes us back out onto the R341 Wild Atlantic Way, heading further along the coast into Connemara land. Connemara is difficult to pinpoint in where it exactly starts and finishes; it's not a town or valley but a rugged and wild part of Galway covering about a third of the county and encompassing the 3,800 acres of Connemara National Park with its heaths, grasslands, only walkways and no roads, herds of red deer, and what I epitomized it for—the beautiful wild, white roaming Connemara ponies and the only horse breed native to Ireland. Legend has it that the breed originated as a result of a number of Arab horses coming ashore from the Spanish Armada shipwreck near Slyne Head and breeding with the smaller native ponies.

Just a few miles down the road from Roundstone, and what was becoming ever more common, Olly's indicator flashes, and soon we're treated to another unexpected wonder at the end of an anonymous lane surrounded by hills encrusted with giant slabs of ancient stone. Like a mirror image, two empty, horse shoe, curved beaches are lying back-to-back. Flour-fine sand, the creamy colour of a Milky Bar, melts into the aquamarine waters, with bright green emerald grasses almost licking the water's edge. Formed by a narrow sand spit that now separates these two bays, they're better known to the locals as Gurteen Bay and Dog's Bay. The reflective bright blue sky further enhances these lost and hidden beaches, and the waters' bold colours could make you think, quite convincingly, you were stranded in the Caribbean! No one else is here with us, except for one mellow guy striking chords from his guitar from the back of his camper van.

Continuing on along the coastal flat, green shore lands, the ever-increasing brown water peat bogs appear like scattered jig-saw pieces with wild yellow irises dotted around everywhere you look. Tiny little bridges lead us over equally tiny seawater estuaries that flow inland to quickly disappear into the permeable lands. And all the time, scatterings of those hand-built stone walls, boats hauled up into fields, thatched white cottages, fresh clear breezes, and more silence.

At Ballyconneely, a tiny spur road takes us down a small peninsula towards Slyne Head, where passing the relics of Bunowen Castle, built around 1500 A.D., and inquisitive white Connemara ponies nuzzling the roadside fences, we come to Grainne Cove and curiously ride our bikes to the very end of Bunowen Pier, jutting out to sea. We've literally come to the end of the track. It's in this cove perched on the water's edge where the Connemara Smokehouse, the oldest one in the area, operates using traditional methods to deliciously smoke salmon, tuna, mackerel, and herrings. We're even told the beaches around here have edible shellfish and molluscs accessible at low tide, including clams, cockles, razorfish, shrimp, and sea urchins.

And with local knowledge and a little help, you may even find the occasional lobster. This place has magnificent views overlooking another relic, the Castle of Grace O'Malley, which proudly stands beside yet another white beach out across these sparkling waters. With the smell of sweet smoke on our clothes and a couple of packs of smoked salmon jammed into our side-panniers, we wave goodbye to the kind people and bump back up onto the small coastal road. The narrow Bog Road, as it's aptly named, on this south coast of Connemara, just before Clifden, feels as bumpy as a sea crossing, but it passes through magical landscapes whose brown peat bogs are honeycombed with thousands of dark black lakes.

Before long, Connemara's capital, the Victorian town of Clifden, appears, and we happily find a convenient and tempting place to stop at in the Market Square for our usual piece of cake and thirst-quenching brew.

Finishing the first of many bites into a guilt-ridden slab of chocolate cake, I clear my throat, "So are we ready to go and ride the Sky Road? This is an iconic road that everyone says has jaw-dropping views and that we just need to follow the signs out of the square here in Clifden."

When early tourists asked where the high road led, local people simply pointed "up towards the sky." And it's been called the Sky Road ever since. Author William Makepeace Thackeray visited the area in 1842—"The Bay and the Reek which sweeps down to the sea and a hundred islands in it, were dressed up in gold and purple and crimson, with the whole cloudy west in a flame." And stories of mermaids or sea-nymphs, known in Ireland as *merrows*, are as old as folklore. Even in the twentieth century, fishermen claim to have seen them among these islands. Sitting combing their green hair on the rocks, they sang to lure sailors to their deaths. Seafarers here regarded them as a sign of shipwreck or gales.

So, the views high up there should be spectacular, and with our luck, with these endless cloudless skies, we should be able to see miles out to sea and around the coast. So, getting back on the bikes, we leave Clifden and start the ten-mile circular Sky Road loop that slowly starts to climb until reaching dizzying heights, with views getting ever bigger. At the very top, we ride into a small parking area that looks out to sea. It's here we witness the spectacular Clew Bay, a natural ocean bay and its incredible 365 "drowned" drumlins, or elongated hills—one island for each day of the year! And one of those islands even belonged to John Lennon up until his death, the uninhabited Dorinish Island, where it was said he shipped in a multicoloured caravan and took both his wives there, wanting to ultimately build a peaceful retreat. And back in 2012 this nineteen-acre island, known more commonly as Beatle Island, was put up for sale for £240,000.

But from where we're standing with the spectacular height and unprotected openness, the wind is starting to pummel us from every side. Perhaps stupidly, and much too confidently, I wheel the bike to the end of the viewpoint for this unique and not-to-be-missed photo opportunity.

And then it happens! An enormous and unexpected gust of wind appears out of nowhere and dramatically blows my bike over. Olly flaps her arms up in sympathetic horror and rushes over. With both of us pushing and pulling, it thankfully stands back up with no external damage, besides a slightly scraped mirror, which doesn't really worry me. But it's when I come to unsuccessfully start the bike that I understand the problem and start slightly panicking. Here we are in one of the remotest places, and I'm potentially stranded. My mind starts to race in over-drive of all the possible consequences, from having to abandon the trip totally to paying masses to get the bike repaired. But there is something positive in that at least Olly's here and she could always as a last resort ride back down into town to get help if there's nothing we can do.

With the fall onto its side, the engine's been badly flooded, and as Olly very wisely and calmly states, "The first thing you should do is stop attempting to start it and let it sit for at least fifteen minutes. This should allow the built-up fuel inside the engine to drain out and then we can be back on the road!"

So, we patiently wait on the side of the road until finally, crossing my fingers, I nervously turn the key, and the beautiful sound of the engine jumps back into life. I almost hug Olly with joy and for me not letting the side down. With a massive sigh of relief, we're off again along this steep and narrow one-lane corniche that twists and turns, heading around to Kingston. We even catch glimpses of the Twelve Bens, a dozen sharp—often mist enshrouded—grey peaks and mostly all within the Connemara Park. Passing roofless, abandoned buildings scattered across the landscape, we later learn, stopping to speak to a guy walking up the road, it was a way of tax avoidance to prove no one lived in them. This also includes a sad looking, old seaweed processing factory that is now empty and long abandoned. We've soon picked up the N59 again and, in a forested setting, shortly come to a crossroads with just a few pubs and B&Bs welcoming us to little Letterfrack, cosily nestled under Diamond Hill and the entranceway into the Connemara Park. It's that time again to look at the maps in the warmth of a little pub. Finally, nodding in agreement and downing our hot chocolates, we wrap up again to brave the last leg of today's journey to Leenane on the shores of Killary Harbour.

On this cold but sunny day with its endless blue skies, the lonely silent road is absolutely spectacular as we pass the neo-Gothic fantasy of Kylemore Abbey and enter the vast green Kylemore Valley with lakes and large inlets of calm waters surrounded by those majestic grey, green, and brown mountains. This massive expanse of water is Killary Fjord, also known as Killary Harbour, and often referred to as Ireland's only natural fjord! It slices more than ten miles inland, and as we see for the first time, enormous expanses and lines of mussel farms cover its surface. Red floating buoys are connected to ropes that are dropped into the cool, still waters where the mussels are attached and left without interference to grow for at least a year.

We continue on through the quiet mountains, lonely moors, and along through this fjord road until we reach the isolated village of Leenane at the head of Killary Fjord. Leenane Hotel looks like one of those old majestic Irish residences with its white washed frontage, its massive stone-floored hallway accommodating umbrellas and boots, countryside paintings depicting local mountain and fishing scenes, walls covered with hunting trophies, and large ornate rooms with welcoming squishy sofas and giant roaring log fires. We both smile, reading each other's minds that "this'll do very nicely!"

We're led up the large curving staircase to our room, but it's here on the silent landing that Olly squeals out in giggles, discreetly nudging me, grabbing my arm, and whispering, "Oh my god, this long, endless corridor with its red carpet looks like we've just arrived at *The Shining* hotel and just about to see Jack!"

But she couldn't have been further from the truth, as this is a wonderful welcoming place, which we'd decided to indulge in and use as our base to explore Connemara over the next few days. That evening, at the hotel's Connemara Seaweed Baths Spa, we experience bathing among and untying ourselves from strings of slippery seaweed! Stepping into the warm sea water bath, a generous helping of seaweed harvested daily from the fjord is floating on the surface, and recommended to be vigorously rubbed all over the body! The salt water is apparently essential for the release of the minerals from this wild seaweed! In my own room, with a ceiling to floor view out to the loch outside, I sink down into the comforting smelling warmth, with the tensions of riding all day and what happened up on that Sky Road mountain slowly disappearing into oblivion.

Later that night, gorged out by the massive potato fest dinner, sitting back on the sofas and cradling G&Ts in front of the enormous peat-laden roaring fireplace, it feels like we have the place all to ourselves. A few casual comments are made like "I can't believe that you dropped some of those spuds on the table, and they brought us even more!" "We've just got to walk to the village tomorrow and try on some of those Aran wool jumpers!"

But all of a sudden, Olly swipes her head like a fly has attacked her. She repeats the motion again and again. I look in curiosity as she quickly jumps up from her seat, and then I look up at the ceiling. A crack has appeared, and water is dripping down in an ever-increasing torrent.

Olly's eyes widen, and she jumps into action, rushing to the front desk. Nobody. She rings the desk bell. No answer.

She runs back to the now drenched sofa. "Goodness me; this isn't good. The ceiling could come down. Maybe someone has left their bath taps on!"

And with that, I watch amusingly as Olly drags the heavy sofa to one side, frantically begins to remove plants from their decorative pots, and then expertly places them under the dripping ceiling, where bigger and longer cracks are beginning to appear. Clapping my hands at this performance almost ensues, but not quite. After what seems like quite a while, a bleary-eyed duty manager casually walks in like this is something not to be too worried about and certainly not an emergency.

"Are you two girls alright? I'll take care of this. We'll be fine. Everything will be sorted by tomorrow."

The next morning at breakfast, Olly takes a sip of tea from her china cup with her pinky in the air and mutters, "You actually swallow them, not eat or chew them!"

I look up from yesterday's *Irish Independent* in surprise. "What do you mean?"

She swizzles her index finger, indicating to be patient while she finishes her mouthful of egg and bacon, and blurts out, "I mean the oysters. That's what you do when you eat them."

I give a look of puzzlement, wanting to potentially contradict that statement but not totally sure. "Well when

I used to live in Paris, the very first time I experienced oysters was at a posh New Year's Eve party in the sixteenth arrondissement, and all the French seemed to be eating them. My French friends always said they ate them mainly because they were aphrodisiacs! I have to say, I've never really been a fan of them with their taste, but today that may change! Our ride over to the Oyster Farm in Ballinakill Bay this morning should reveal everything. Want to take a gamble on swallow or chew? The winner can get the drinks in tonight!"

Olly smiles and nods her head as she generously spreads yet more marmalade on her thick toast and Irish scones, "And what's the news from Ireland's perspective today?"

I look back down at yesterday's 13th May 2019 newspaper. It's the first time I'd really seen any news since we'd arrived, and it's felt fairly pleasant and liberating that we've lost track of anything from the outside world, which we both agreed was nearly always bad news anyway.

I sigh with boredom, "It's all about Brexit." I'll read a bit . . . "'May's time runs short. And no-deal Brexit still looms! It has dropped off the news agenda for the last three weeks. But it has not gone away—in fact, it has gone nowhere at all. Yes, Brexit remains very much with us. And as the time ticks inexorably down to the new deadline of October 31, 2019, the stalemate in the United Kingdom has worsened. Theresa May is under increasing pressure inside her own Conservative Party to resign. The embattled and ill-starred prime minister, rated by many as the worst performing holder of that office in many decades, has already said she will not lead her party into the next general election.'"

Olly also sighs, and I continue, "'Meanwhile, a rather cock-a-hoop Mr. Farage has pumped up demands that the UK leaves the EU without a deal. That would harm Britain and other close trading partners like the Netherlands, France and Germany. But it would be an economic nightmare for Ireland, north and south, with the threat of some nasty political fallout over the Border. So, the spectre of a no-deal Brexit continues to bedevil us—we have just been hearing less about it for a time.'"

This time, I close the paper for good and clap my hands. "Come on! Let's get our helmets and take a ride to see who wins the bet!"

We walk into the grand hallway, and from underneath a wall of taxidermied salmon encased in old decorative glass mounted boxes, we take our helmets and jackets. Like VIPs, or VIMs (Very Important Motorcycles!), the two bikes are parked conveniently just outside the main door, and soon the engines are ripping out the silence from this place. Another unusually warm, sunny day which will top tywenty degrees! The ride back towards Letterfrack is sublime, with its wide, open empty spaces. And not before too long, we've headed off from the main N59 road and, on this single-track, are greeted by thick roadside hedges of bright candy pink and lip-smacking purple rhododendrons, which go on for ever and ever. The track gets ever narrower and ever more gritty and uneven as we pass derelict cottages and tiny inlets of water across the wild, flat land. And it's here I experience the real agility of my new lower bike, feeling a lot more confident than had I been riding the heavy Bonneville.

And this is ever more apparent, as we turn onto a new track, this time covered and magically made up totally from pure white oyster shells! With the tyres crackling the track underneath, it feels like we're riding over a giant Crunchie Bar! The image is so beautiful as the pure white, silvery pathway continues on, leading us around a hidden bend. It's here we've come to the end of the "Oyster Track" and to Ballinakill Bay and one of the best oyster farms in the country, DK Connemara Oysters, where they've been farmed since 1893. We're greeted by a smiling Chris, who over the next hour or so shows us around and teaches us all about the mystery and life of oysters.

Originally, the oysters were taken from here by horse and cart in barrels to Clifden, then they would travel by rail to

Dublin for shipment on the mail boat to England. Today, as Chris explains, "They're still served in our local hotels and restaurants but also exported worldwide with ninety per cent of that for the French market, as the Frenchies like big ones! So, girls let's now walk over to the oyster beds in the seashore over there, where you'll see the rows of oysters that are grown over a three-year period from seed to plate."

He expertly hoists one of the heavy, metal weaved bags out of the water. "Our oysters enjoy a unique habitat in this sheltered bay. So just to let you know, our oysters feed on the phytoplankton carried in by the various currents of the Atlantic Ocean. These currents originate with the Gulf Stream in the warm climate of Florida, forming the western and northern sections of the subtropical North Atlantic Gyre. You'll never believe it but it takes 1,000 years for these currents to replenish and complete their cycle, and they greatly affect the salinity and temperature of our waters in the bay. So, these plankton are microscopic plants and require nitrate and phosphate to grow. These nutrients are the fertilizers of the sea, and the North Atlantic Ocean is one of the most fertile in the world. These shallow, pristine waters of our Ballinakill Bay provide an optimum depth for the growth of the plankton. The minerals provided by the Connemara hills also fertilise these waters, providing our oysters with a rich and healthy food source to ensure their optimum growth. You could say they have a unique taste, as these surrounding hills are home to the famous Connemara lamb, their flavour infused by the same flora and nutrients which influence our sandbanks and, therefore, also giving our oysters their amazing taste! With that, we need to go back to the shed and taste some!"

Before long, Olly is wearing an industrial, blue rubber glove on her left hand and given what looks like a sharp-looking dagger in the other. In front of her is a table of generous sized oysters ready to be opened and consumed by my stoic friend and yours truly.

Chris continues patiently, "So, simply pick up one of the oysters with your gloved hand, and with the knife, insert it between the shell's crack and twist open. Then with the knife gently loosen the oyster from the shell, and you're ready to eat it!"

At that point, Olly looks at me and then back at Chris. "When you say eat it. What do you mean exactly? Do I chew it or swallow it?"

Chris chuckles. having probably heard that same question asked many times before. "Well that's an easy one. You need to savour its incredible taste. so you really need to chew on it."

I think I may have partially won that bet! So after more than our fair share of mastering our oyster opening abilities and eating the whole plateful, we shake hands with Chris. who then waves us goodbye as we vanish down the bumpy shell-strewn lane. Passing the rhododendrons, a pointy mountain rears up at the end of the road, which is our point of reference for where we're headed to next.

Just a few miles outside Letterfrack, we already turn off again and ride down a private road to the 15,000 acre estate of Kylemore Abbey, which most people and books we've read say is the number one "Must-See" attraction in western Ireland. It was back in the 1860s when it was first created as a dream home by industry tycoon and pioneer Mitchell Henry.

This photogenic nineteenth century neo-Gothic fantasy, still accommodating nuns and with its own Benedictine church, is perched on grassy banks to perfectly mirror its greyish-white stone frontage onto the waters of Pollacapall Lough. We don't waste time loitering or meandering behind the other visitors, but head directly through the tree-lined avenues to the extravagant Victorian walled gardens, with that same pointy mountain rearing its head on the other side of the valley. The barren Connemara boglands to the west of the castle were transformed into what was recognised at the time as Ireland's most impressive walled garden, covering a massive six acres. Vegetables and fruits of every kind are still being grown here within the shelter of the red brick walls, smothered in tied-back fruit trees dazzling with their colourful pink and white spring blossoms. Gardening was and still is taken seriously here with the old and beautiful Head Gardener's House, the stone Bothy—or basic accommodation for the garden boys—and ornate Glass Houses nestled in this area, which have been beautifully and patiently restored. Now no longer used but on display, furnished and decorated as they originally looked, these buildings were an essential part of the estate all those years ago.

The road to Leenane, with its yellow gorse and purple rhododendrons, leads us back into the wilderness, but not quite. In the total isolation we're forced to practice a quick emergency practice stop! Out in front of us on this desolate road, a large barrelled lorry—maybe carrying milk—has literally fallen off the road and is precariously balancing sideways on its side and six right-side wheels. But this is Ireland, and there's no panic. The driver is casually standing by the road, with both hands in his pockets while quietly looking out to the horizon. We both stop to see if help is needed; not that we'd have the strength to push it back up!

I pull up my visor and kindly smile, "Good afternoon to you. Is there anything we can do?"

The stocky, white-haired driver simply smiles back and in a thick Irish accent replies, "Oh, no, everything is just fine, ladies. Another big truck will be here at some time today to get this lorry pulled back up. I'm happy that it's a sunny day. It's the real ting! But thank you for asking. Have a good day." And with that, he kindly waves us goodbye.

Just up the road, I pull into a lay-by to tighten my chin strap, and park up next to a large solitary sign attached to a stone wall, which simply says "Stop and Pray." Out in this vast, peaceful openness it seems a perfect place to see such a sign. I look back at the driver and his truck and put out a prayer that he'll be collected soon and that all other fellow travellers, including us, will be kept safe.

Connemara is exceeding all my expectations with its beauty and warmest of welcomes, and later that night, we're in for another treat. After a sumptuous meal, we slowly head towards the bar for a whiskey nightcap while listening to captivating traditional music from a three-piece local Irish band playing their banjo and Irish pipes. The setting is perfect, but soon that's all about to change. All of a sudden, the musicians change tempo and start playing and singing French music! Both Olly and I look at each other quizzically, but our questions are soon answered. Two large buses have arrived, and more than fifty French people walk into the bar area and overflow, forcing a number of French women to sit politely on chairs all in a row in the hallway! We're perplexed on the choice of music, without the guests even enthusiastic enough to tap their feet, clap, or sing along but conclude that this is maybe the Irish way of welcoming the French.

We're back out on the bikes bright and early the next day to ride over to the Connemara National Park, which once formed part of the Kylemore Abbey estate we'd visited the day before. In the past, the park lands were used for agriculture, mainly as grazing for cattle and sheep, and vegetables were grown on some of the more fertile lowlands. Not surprisingly, as we're beginning to see, the bogs here were used extensively to dig up peat as fuel sources. Now it covers 2,000 hectares of scenic mountains, expanses of bogs, heaths, grasslands, and woodlands. Some of the park's mountains, namely Benbaun, Bencullagh, Benbrack, and Muckanaght, are part of the famous Twelve Bens, or Beanna Beola range. The park was established and opened to the public in 1980 and is open all year round. With no through roads for any sort of vehicle, it's a walker's paradise with hundreds of trails.

With helmets in hand and heavy apparel weighing us down, we stoically stagger up and along the ever-heightening trail with its white Connemara ponies grazing silently up into the heather clad hillsides. After just a short while, we both turn around to look at each other's slightly reddened faces. We're both out of breath, sighing heavily, slightly sweaty under the armpits, and so unanimously decide the only sensible course of action is to simply turn back! Our throats are parched so it's not long before heading back that we make a stop at the "Misunderstood Heron," a well-known wooden trailer parked up on the roadside serving delicious cheese and leek pasties, cakes, and coffee. Sitting on the grassy verge, we also eat up the jaw-dropping views extending out over the fjord, the floating mussel farms, the purple rhododendron bushes, the yellow gorse bushes, and the white blossoming hawthorn trees, and all warmly hugged by the mountains around us and the sunshine above us. Decidedly exhausted from the fresh air, we head back under the bright blue skies with wispy clouds, along the lovely twisting and long stretches of roads, passing the odd timber truck and the occasional waving biker.

With no more flooded ceilings or French singing to sort out or contend with, we're up with the dawn chorus the next morning for the next leg of the trip into County Mayo and the northern coastal peninsulas. But we can't get away that quickly, as a group of elderly French gentlemen have congregated and are quizzically looking over and examining our bikes. A group gasp comes out of their mouths when they see us girls walk over putting our helmets on. The bus driver is a friendly enough guy, and as his French passengers are loading up and getting seated, he kindly suggests that we should leave now to get a good head start away from him. This can only mean one thing in my mind's eye—that the road might be fairly challenging, narrow, and it might be difficult to overtake anything.

And it's yet another unbelievably sunny, clear, and cloudless day that many Irish would definitely say is not the norm, but we're happy with that! Maybe we've been given the luck of the Irish! So, off we start through Leenane, but no sooner have we left do we the make a pit-stop in front of a pub with its beer barrels stacked on the pavement. We're not stopping to take a drink but to fill up our bikes, as it also serves as a petrol station! We continue riding out and along, the sheep grazing water's edge where we see and feel midges for the first time, past the long rows of mussel beds and rhododendron-lined roads and turn a sharp left up and around to the other side of Killary sea inlet to look out to where we'd just come from. Our little white Leenane Hotel now looks just like a little speck in the landscape, huddled into the hillside.

The small R335 soon leaves the water's edge and heads inland to the luscious Delphi Valley of mountains, where the skies are now becoming ever more overcast, with darkening clouds quickly starting to gather. But if nothing else, it feels strangely and pleasantly warm. And with luck on our side, we manage to escape the rain until early in the evening. But it's also here that we make a quick stop to fully zip up our jackets to shield us from the blustery winds and ever-increasing chill. The lonely, reed-lined Doo Lough—The Dark Lake—with grass covered mountains towering over it and plunging into its still waters, appears on our left. In its middle we both point to a solitary rowing boat with two stoic fishermen patiently biding their time.

As we contentedly continue riding, the mountains die away and the road slowly climbs, bringing us out onto open, wild heather-covered moorland. At the top of one of the many crests, a solitary but familiar looking tourist bus is parked up on the side of the road. Standing next to it is the same group of French men I'm sure we'd seen at the hotel looking at our bikes earlier this morning. They're sharply tuning their ears to the sound of our motorcycle engines approaching them and then point wildly and excitedly at us. They're seeing us in action now! As we approach and nod to say bonjour, they also theatrically wave back and, twisting their clenched fists, shout out "brummmm! brummmm!" I snigger under my helmet and obey by twisting my throttle to accelerate even faster past them!

Across the murky, brown boglands, thousands upon thousands of black peat turf bricks lay out in hundreds of lines or stand up in conical piles to dry out. People here each own small patches of this bogland, where they can freely dig up the peat for use in heating their homes. Once these bricks have dried, someone will no doubt soon be coming to collect them. The same twisting road, with its grazing donkeys, reaches the shore again at Louisburgh and heads eastwards to Westport, where we stop at silent Westport Quay in search of another elusive tea shop. Just one will do! But all effort is futile. So, we continue up along the quiet N59 until the pretty little eighteenth century village of Newport appears after we've crossed over the beautiful seven-arch viaduct on the Newport River. The bikes are conveniently parked outside Kelly's Kitchen on another Main Street, and we enter this small tea shop strangely displaying a giant photograph of Grace Kelly! We look questioningly at each other but shrug our shoulders, with no clear answer, and walk to the counter to place our orders.

Shortly afterwards, a smiling waitress in a flowery pinafore brings us bowls of delicious local seafood chowder. I look up enquiringly at the photograph of Grace on the wall, and the waitress nods, "Yes, it's for sure! Grace Kelly has family connections going a long way back to Newport. That's why we love her here so much! You're going to love County Mayo. It's a well-kept secret and without the crowds!"

And telling her where we're headed, she continues, "Oh for sure! The village of Keel on Achill Island is the island's main hub of activity!" As we see later on, the word *activity* is a purely relative term! Through Newport we continue out along and through fields, with a glimpse of Clew Bay and its many islands until we reach the quaint village of Mulrany, high over a sandy coastal strip looking out to sea with views out to Clare Island. The road hugs the sea to Achill Sound, where the little bridge takes us finally to Achill.

Ireland's largest offshore island, Achill is linked to the mainland by a short bridge but, despite the accessibility, still has that immediate remote-island feel as we turn onto "Atlantic Drive." Achill Island, as we quickly see, is virtually unknown to visitors and is even quite often forgotten in tourist guides about Ireland. There are breath-taking views down, over a wild rocky bay . . . around a fine scenic cork screw road. and the barren mountains slowly become greener with long-haired sheep and their prancing lambs all over the place. Passing through one of the small settlements, I can't help but smile when I see an aproned woman with a broom chasing sheep out of her front garden! The place seems like an Instagram haven, if you're into that sort of stuff, with photo opportunities every few minutes. With everything we were seeing for the first time, we were lucky if we were exceeding speeds to keep the bikes upright!

All over Achill, the terrain bears the scars of a striped landscape from years of cutting turf, whose traditional cutting methods have not changed for many generations and with the skills still passed down from family to family. Every spring, the turfcutter "scrawed" the bog by cutting away the surface of vegetation on the turf bank and then cutting the turf into "sods" using a slean. The slean is a special spade for turf cutting, and the brick-shape cut sods are thrown up onto the bank or into the logphortach. The sods are then left for at least a week to dry before being spread apart. After a week or two, the spread turf is "footed" by stacking them into pyramids of four to six sods, allowing the air to circulate around them. Following a few more weeks, the dry sods are put to one side to leave the others to dry, and then finally the turfs are left to season for another two to three weeks before being taken away to heat homes. Nowadays, most of the turf is apparently cut by machine, but the same process of manually working and saving the turf is still the same as generations ago.

We'd agreed before checking into our Airbnb place in Keel West that we'd head out to hidden Keem Bay before it got dark and, more importantly, before it started to slash down with rain. This is one of Ireland's remotest beaches on its furthest western tip; some would also say one of the best beaches anywhere so that it's earned a Blue Flag status. As we ascend, the road becomes increasingly narrower, until it feels like we're riding high up along a secret pathway through the hills. This is what I'd call a very advanced rider's road, without any barrier and the cliff right next to the track dropping straight into the Atlantic, which is crashing violently over the rocks far, far below. It's just a little bit scary. I gulp, thankful this time of riding this lighter bike with the ease and safety of putting my feet flat on the floor. Even so, I still feel we'd better just concentrate and look straight ahead, without stopping to take silly photos or have a natter!

But finally, at the top of the track the views become even more spectacular looking down to this lost little cove. All we need do now is hang on tight and spiral down to this perfect hideaway with its clear green waters and golden sands. Finally letting out a deep sigh of relief that we've safely made it all the way down, we take a long walk along the quiet, wild beach, with almost no one else in sight, and look out to sea for those elusive dolphins. The surrounding cliffs and hills feel like they're shielding the bay from the wind, which strangely makes the whole place feel a lot warmer than where we've just come from.

The ride back up the steep hill feels a lot easier, and the only vehicles we encounter are a few "off the grid" wild camper vans, already parked up off the track for the night. Riding through the empty streets of Keel, we find the address and park up behind a house overlooking the sea. A cosy little cottage at the back will be ours for the night, as a crew-cut teenager smiles and hands us our keys. Right now, though, we still need to search for a place to eat, which means getting back on the bikes in the now cold and drizzling rain. The only place we find open is a pub a few miles down the road, the Gielty's Bar in Dooagh. Known as the last pub on the road of pubs in Achill Island and advertised as the "Most Westerly Pub in Europe," we're only grateful it's serving any sort of food at this late hour! But not for the first time, the place, although totally empty except for one bloke and his dog, is welcoming us with blazing peat fires and a warm smile from the girl behind the bar.

Slowly sipping our dark black Guinness, we smile in recognition with the coincidence and spontaneously start tapping our feet to Ireland's leading country singer, Nathan Carter, who's melodically blasting out from a radio at the back of the bar—

Another turning point a fork stuck in the road.
Time grabs you by the wrist directs you where to go
So, make the best of this test and don't ask why
It's not a question but a lesson learned in time
It's something unpredictable but in the end it's right
I hope you've had the time of your life
So, take the photographs and still frames in your mind
Hang it on a shelf in good health and good time
Tattoos and memories and good skin on trial
For what it's worth it was worth it all the while
It's something unpredictable but in the end it's right
I hope you've had the time of your life

And with that, we hungrily tuck into delicious and tender, roasted Achill Lamb, raised in the nearby Salt Flats—heather sweetened and seaside seasoned. The habitual giant serving of delicious creamy mashed potato, which we've found accompanies almost every meal here in Ireland, is heaped onto our plates as we smile, having accomplished yet another incredibly unique day out on the Irish roads!

The rain pelted down during the night, and after brewing up a coffee and eating fresh croissant with homemade jam, we peer out of our little window. The bikes are soaked, which means only one thing. They'll need a good wipe over, and we'll need to pull our waterproofs on. Fortunately, the rain has stopped, but the skies are miserably grey, and we get that gut feel that an extra layer or two wouldn't go amiss! As we go to leave, Bella, the hosts' brown and white collie, jumps excitedly up at us with her toy frog. Olly pulls it out of her mouth and randomly chucks it down the lane, where Bella, wagging tail and barking excitedly, chases after it.

Before immediately leaving Achill Island, there is just one place we're both curious to make a special detour for and visit—The Deserted Village at Slievemore. Cutting through vast moorland with a wall of black mountains on the horizon and long-haired sheep meandering past us on this tiny road dotted with beds of wild yellow irises, we come to a little intersection. A large, white statue of the Virgin Mary stands alone in this stark moorland, in total contrast to the hundreds of grey gravestones surrounding her and creeping up the slopes. With the blackening early morning grey sky and the misty covered hills, this gives the place a much more melodramatic feel. We leave the bikes parked up with the Virgin Mary and walk towards the remnants of The Deserted Village.

The strange, abandoned village consists of some eighty to one hundred derelict and roofless stone cottages located along a mile-long stretch of road on the southern slopes of this remote Slievemore mountain. While some of these dwellings were occupied as summer "booley" homes within living memory, the area itself is rich in archaeological artefacts, including megalithic tombs dating from the Neolithic period, some 5,000 years ago! From a board we read that it seems that site remnants have shown that settlement in this area dates from at least early Medieval times. It's all a bit bleak for my liking but is certainly a strong reminder of the island's past hardships and a vanished way of life. When the Potato Famine—crop failures caused by late blight, a disease destroying the entire potato plant—took hold, starting in 1845 and ending in 1849, starvation forced the villagers to fishing, and the graveyard shows the sad outcome. Slievemore is the largest and most recently abandoned "booley" settlement on Achill, which refers to the practice of living in different locations during the summer and winter periods to allow cattle to graze the summer pastures. By the time we get back, a group of purple spray-painted sheep are quietly grazing around the bikes before seeing us and scampering off!

We duplicate the ride back onto the mainland, and over the bridge jump onto our friend, the N59, to continue heading northwards. Riding through yet another quiet place, this time Ballycroy, my indicators come on, and Olly also stops behind me to park the bikes up along the main street. Helmets come off, with sweaty hair underneath, and we look up and down to see what's open.

"I'm dying for a cup of coffee or anything warm to put my hands around."

Olly nods, "Yes, I thought the same thing too. Nothing much seems to be open, except for that fish and chip shop over the road. Shall we give it a go?"

Walking into the quiet fish and chip shop, a man behind the counter wipes his hands down a white apron after cutting potatoes. "What can we do for you today?"

"Well it's a bit early for your fish and chips, but do you serve tea or coffee and maybe a cake or even just a biscuit?"

He nods, "Yes, of course! It's quiet most of the time here, so we need to be fairly flexible with what we provide, and so most of the day in the morning and afternoon we're just a café."

I continue peering over the counter, looking at the newly cut piles of potatoes ready to be thrown into the sizzling frying pan and turned into chips, and chirp up by saying, "Ireland really is the place for potatoes, isn't it? You must never have a shortage to make your lovely chips!"

He laughs out, like I've just made the joke of the century, and startles us with what he goes on to say, "Well not really! The Irish import the Maris Piper potatoes from Cambridgeshire, because they're big and perfect for making fat chips. Our potatoes are smaller and mainly used just for Mah-mee's mash dinners!"

We both look back with incredulity in learning this amazing fact. Who would have thought! Replenished from starvation by buying a few pies and cakes from him, we continue up past the Ballycroy National Park to the little village of Bangor, where it's here the road spikes onto the R313 and onto the Mullet Peninsula. Without a doubt, the feeling of increasing and total isolation is apparent the further we continue. This Gaeltacht (mainly Irish-speaking) peninsula dangles itself some twenty-odd miles out into the Atlantic, and most of the time the only other traffic we see are stubborn sheep forever blocking the road. It's sparsely populated, with just small numbers of cottages dotted across the landscape. The only settlement of any significance is Belmullet, where we religiously fill our tanks at a garage opposite a beautiful statue of the white Madonna, once again representing the strong, religious communities and beliefs held here in Ireland.

Finally, we can go no further and arrive at the end of a road in Blacksod Bay, where a stone lighthouse stands. We turn up another little road, past a few fields, and ride down a driveway of a large, solitary detached house, which will be our place for the next couple of nights. There's nothing else around us, and it has that end-of-the-earth appea,l which makes us feels like we've found the remotest accommodation possible in Ireland! But not for the first time, the welcome is once again a warm one, and we're shown to our room, even if we feel the hostess is possibly a little neurotic when she questions if we'll be lying on her nicely made beds with our biking gear on. Ten minutes later, when we've changed into more feminine and cleanish attire, she withdraws her statement and quickly smiles in reassurance.

Sitting in the kitchen with a cup of tea and the obligatory thick-buttered scone, the first of many questions blurt out to Hannah, "So what's the best thing we can do here?"

She thinks that question over like it's the most difficult mastermind question ever asked in history, "Well, . . . well, . . . I know! You could maybe walk to the pier, where a few fishing boats may be moored up. You can have a look at the lighthouse. You might even bump into Vincent, the lighthouse keeper, while you're here, who could show you round it. That's about it."

Olly encouragingly nods for more information, "That's good! And where can we buy some food or go to eat?"

"Well, there are no shops here. You'd have to go all the way back to Belmullet. But I'll be making you breakfast here, which is very filling, and our café may be open tomorrow, but again, that's not for sure! If needs be, I've got some baked beans in the cupboard I can heat up and put on toast for you tonight!"

I look at Olly and smile, liking this situation of spontaneity we've created for ourselves. "Why don't we stretch our legs and amble down to the pier and see if any fishing boats have come in. It's high tide, so they should have. Might be interesting."

Without any other obvious options to suggest, Olly obligingly nods and follows me out of the house and down the lane. Towards the pier, which has a handful of white commercial trucks parked up alongside it, and passing some rusty round containers lying in deep grass, we stop to look at several beautiful long currachs lying upside down, revealing their black tarred canvas hulls. Looking more like rowing boats or similar to the River Thames skiffs back in England, we guess they're probably used here for rowing out to sea to do some fishing or maybe ferrying fishermen to the larger fishing boats when they're not moored up beside the pier. I'd heard of currach racing too, so maybe these were also competitive vessels! Opposite the pier and across the road is the granite lighthouse that looks securely locked up with no visible sign of life from within.

But there is a little notice on a wall, which we read with interest, from *The Irish Times* in 1865—"I arrived at the pier of Blacksod Bay and observed a very handsome lighthouse in the course of erection. I was struck with the beauty of the granite, and at first sight I thought it must have been imported from Wales or Dalkey. I asked who the contractor was, and where he got the splendid granite. I was told that the granite was got on the shores here. I then inquired of the stone masons whether this or the Dalkey granite was the best. They replied 'There is no comparison as the Blacksod Bay granite. All the granite along the shore is cut out by nature into all sizes rendering them fit for window stools, window sills or pillars of fifteen to twenty feet long and simply raised by crowbars out of their beds, as the whole upper and lower strata are cut by seams.' My next enquiry was to the facilities of transport and the loading of vessels of heavy tonnage. I found out that vessels of any tonnage could come up to within twenty yards of the shore; and that this bay is one of the safest in Ireland in stormy weather for vessels to run into."

In fact, so good was this stone that granite from Blacksod was exported to all parts of Europe and England at the end of the nineteenth century, including helping to build London's Houses of Parliament and 10 Downing Street!

We wander down and along the pier where at the end are three red and white, fairly large fishing boats moored and tied up horizontally, side by side. Besides a couple of fishermen sweeping the decks clean on the boat nearest the wall, there's nothing much else going on. It looks like all the fish may have already been taken away in those white trucks we saw earlier, so that's an event we've missed. But, out of curiosity, I peer down deep into the nearest boat's hull, and besides an empty plastic barrel, a drill, and a lost shoe, I see an incredible sight—a box full of massive crab claws and one giant turbot. Why are they there? The fisherman below on the same deck looks up and smiles. I do likewise, wave, and feel it would be rude not to start some sort of conversation.

Not really knowing the correct terminology, I simply ask, "So, have you had a good outing?"

The waterproof clad fisherman nods, "We could have done better, but the buyers were happy in what they took. We'll see what tomorrow's fishing brings."

Still thinking about sourcing some sort of food for tonight, I excitedly and in a daredevil sort of way ask, "Why are all those crab claws there? Are any for sale?"

He chuckles, "Oh those! We don't want those. We have them every day, and enough is enough!"

I bravely continue, "So would it be at all possible to maybe buy a few from you? We've got nothing for dinner, besides baked beans!"

He looks at me in wonderment at what I've just said and reaches down to the box. "You must be joking! You can have them all for nothing plus the turbot! They probably would have been thrown out for the gulls. I'll grab some plastic bags from the cabin."

With that, he disappears, and Olly taps me on the shoulder and with her wide-open eyes, I see her silent mouth discreetly form the shapes to say something like "I can't believe it!"

Robbie appears again and stuffs two supermarket bags full to breaking point of giant crab claws and the speckled brown and white turbot, which is so fresh it's still moving. Money is again offered and again refused. That simple act of generosity touches us, and we kindly wave him goodbye as we excitedly run back to the B&B!

Olly speaks without stopping for breath, "We'll need to ask Hannah if we can use her kitchen to cook everything, so we can eat it later on. I hope it's not a problem, but this is incredible and something totally unexpected, and way better than those old baked beans!"

When we open the bags and show Hannah, her jaw drops in total disbelief and becomes even more hyper. "How on earth did you do that? If you two girls landed in a bucket of shite, I bet you'd still come up smelling o' roses! I've been trying for years and never got anything like that from the fishermen. You'll need to go into the outside kitchen, where you can boil the claws in my big pans, and I'll be happy to cook your fish, but it needs to be gutted first."

It's then we feel a little guilty, feeling we're possibly overtaking the situation, having only arrived a few hours ago, and so Olly chirps up, "That's so kind. You're more than welcome to have some of these claws and some of the fish, as this is more than enough for us."

Hannah smiles and eagerly nods as we see her almost licking her lips, "Well if you insist. My husband's coming back later tonight, so a few of those claws would be most welcome!"

I look back at the Turbot and back to Olly, "You do know that one of us is going to have to put it out of its misery. I can't stand it anymore."

Olly smiles nervously and asks Hannah for something she can use. A large, stone pestle is produced, and Hannah and I hide behind Olly while she massacres and clubs to death our dinner.

Hannah re-appears from behind Olly. "But I do know someone who could come to gut the fish. It's Vincent from the lighthouse and who lives just up the road. Let me give him a call to see if he can come over now."

Hardly ten minutes later, a little demure man in his sixties politely walks into the kitchen and smiles, looking at the crazy proceedings of boiling water saucepans covering the entire hob and what's on the chopping board. "That is a gorgeous fish. I was a charter fishing man for twenty years, so I should know! That'll make a good meal with some nice salad and mash!"

Introductions are made, and Vincent demonstrates putting the crab claws in the pans. They're all so fresh that they seem to still be moving in the water! Just a few minutes and they're done. He then pulls out a sharp knife from his bag slung over his shoulder and leans seriously over the big fish to prepare it for tonight's dinner. Laughs and banter are exchanged in this strange setting, and after a while, everything has been prepared.

Vincent makes a dash for the door, saying that he's forgotten some bread cooking in his oven, but turns and mutters, "Girls, I'll be at the lighthouse tomorrow, so I could show you around it. How does eleven sound?"

We gratefully smile for another unexpected, kind gesture and keenly put our thumbs up to accept his invitation. The lighthouse isn't normally open to the public, so we're feeling pretty honoured.

That evening, we dine like kings, with Hannah even unearthing a couple of bottles of beer for us and some fresh lemon to squeeze over the banquet. The crab is so tender, moist, and delicious and the turbot a real treat. But even with hungry stomachs we don't manage to eat half the feast, so we're pleased to know what we'll be having tomorrow, without the need to go out shopping! Our experiences of surprises today certainly didn't come in half-measures but once again full to the top with extra helpings of kindness and generosity.

At eleven hundred hours, precisely, on Saturday morning, Vincent is outside Blacksod Lighthouse rummaging away in his pockets for a massive set of keys. "Well good morning girls! I hope the fish was good last night. I've got a bit of tracking and monitoring to do here, so there's a bit of time to show you around."

The thick, heavy, storm-proof metal door is opened, and Vincent politely directs us into what initially and surprisingly looks just like a shuttered-up, two-storey little house with bedrooms, a kitchen, and an office plastered with maritime maps all over the walls. "Yes, I know what you're thinking. The rooms are a good size, and it feels like a house. I grew up as a kid here with my parents and it was our family home for a long time, so I really don't know any other life. But this place has a lot of stories to tell, if only the walls could talk! It's actually only one of two square-shaped lighthouses in Europe; the other one's in Germany. The lighthouse keeper here is responsible for the Blackrock Lighthouse too, out on Blackrock Island, which is located northwest of Achill Island and about twelve miles west of us here at Blacksod Bay."

He continues, "Back in the past, this lighthouse was the last thing a lot of people saw leaving Ireland for a new life! Steamers set off from Blacksod Bay on fifteen voyages to Boston or Quebec in 1883-84. Each family among the 3,300 passengers on board received free clothing, travel, and money towards their new life, thanks to an incredible person, the Quaker James Hack Tuke. He spent over sixty years trying to eradicate poverty here in the west of Ireland. We still see descendants returning to visit this spot where their families embarked all those years ago!"

With that, he quietly sighs and leads us up the narrow circular stairs to the top of the tower and into the small conical lantern section, where the rotating light stands. Crouching through a small opening in the wall, we walk onto the open platform surrounding the tower with its unrestricted 360-degree views out to sea. We lean against the thick, protective stone wall and look out into the distance across the waters to Achill Island and the open Atlantic waters beyond. Below us is the harbour with its bobbing fishing boats and behind us the emergency helicopter landing pad for the twenty-four hour search and rescue air ambulances. The chilly wind is stroking our faces, and I pull my beanie hat down over my ears.

"If you look down there, you'll see the walls around the lighthouse that have been rebuilt. In 1989 a massive rogue wave came in and badly damaged and destroyed all the walls. Something we'd never seen before."

Olly chirps up, "We really want to hear all about things and life here."

For a moment Vincent pauses then smiles looking out to sea and starts to tell more than one incredible story to us. "It was really my father, Ted Sweeney, who had a major part to play in the history here. Before the opening of the meteorological station at Carne in 1957, he provided weather information from Blacksod to Dublin. My father's weather forecast in June 1944 delayed the D-Day invasion of Normandy by Allied troops, by one day! You could say this lighthouse changed the entire course of the Second World War!"

We look in disbelief and nod, urging him to continue. And with that, we feel he's being swept away in time " . . . Blacksod, Blacksod calling . . . here's the weather report for June 3rd, 1944!—In the history of mankind, few weather forecasts have carried such significance. As my father cranked the telephone and delivered this news over a crackly line from here, which is County Mayo's most westerly point, he had no idea the lives of more than 150,000 Allied troops would hang on his very words.

"It was a fateful call. As he watched the barometer fall precipitously, Ted's report from here, the Coast Guard station, ultimately convinced General D. Eisenhower to delay the D-Day invasion for twenty-four hours and a decision we later found out averted a military catastrophe and changed the course of the Second World War! And it was the Blacksod forecast here that changed everything. Years of planning for the Allied invasion came down to one crucial but uncontrollable factor—the weather. Everyone was involved to get it as accurate as possible, including observations from the RAF, the Royal Navy, and American Air Force meteorologists. But the forecast from Blacksod here on the Mullet peninsula was vital. This was because it was the first land-based observation station in Europe where readings could be taken on prevailing Atlantic westerly weather systems. Despite Ireland's neutrality, it did continue to send reports to Britain under arrangements since Independence, but these were not passed on to Germany.

"D-Day was originally planned for June 5, as tide conditions were deemed ideal for seaborne and airborne landings. But as the day of the greatest invasion in history approached, the forecasters couldn't agree on the forecasted weather for that day. There was a serious dilemma. Then just after 2AM on June 3, my father sent his latest hourly weather observation report, and it contained an ominous warning of a Force 6 wind and a rapidly falling barometer at Blacksod. At Southwick House outside

Portsmouth, Group Captain Stagg studied the Blacksod report and strongly advised General Eisenhower to postpone the invasion by twenty-four hours, which would bring clearer weather from the Atlantic. Nine hours later the telephone rang again, and a lady with an English accent requested a repeat of the last weather observations my father had sent earlier, and which he again repeated. This request for a check happened again an hour later to repeat the same weather observations. He was wondering what was wrong. He thought he'd made an error or something like that. It never dawned on him that this was the weather for invading or anything like that. When he checked the report and knew it was correct, he thanked God that he'd done his job and sent the correct reading to London.

"Then at 12PM on June 4, my father sent another report that offered hope to Eisenhower to launch Overlord. It reported— heavy rain and drizzle cleared, cloud at 900 feet and visibility on land and sea very clear. In the early hours of the following day, at Eisenhower's morning briefing, the latest report from us at Blacksod confirmed the passage of a cold front. A loud cheer went up in the room. Complete confidence was restored, and Eisenhower's long-awaited weather clearance had finally arrived, and he gave the order for Overlord to proceed. D-Day would definitely be on June 6. Some 5,000 ships and over 11,000 aircraft carried approximately 156,000 Allied troops into battle on D-Day across a sixty-mile beachfront and into France."

A moment of silence and quiet reflection ensues while by now Olly's hat and scarf have almost hidden her face from the blasting wind. We walk around the tower to the other side and look down at the helicopter pad, where it almost seems that Vincent is sadly remembering a totally different story. We walk back around to look back out to sea and far beyond Achill Island.

Vincent sighs and speaks in a tone of high emotion, "This place is the eyes for the sea. Something really bad happened here just over two years ago on 14 March 2017. There are four

Irish Sea rescue helicopters which patrol our waters; the 115 Shannon, 116 Dublin, 117 Waterford, and 118 Sligo. There was a terrible accident with one of these helicopters. The 116 hit the lighthouse rocks on Blackrock. It's a rocky island rising to a height of seventy metres above sea level. All four of the Irish coast guards perished in the crash. I was the last person to speak to them. I'd only just spoken to them before the helicopter hit that lighthouse out at sea. We think they were seeking to refuel here, as there were no refuelling services at Blackrock, but they must have got confused with the low-lying clouds and were in fact some thirteen kilometres west and flying low enough to crash into the high Blackrock island."

We grip the steep, winding rails back down and shake hands with Vincent to warmly thank this wonderful man for his precious time and wave goodbye but know it probably won't be the last time we see him, as this place is so small! We stride back past Hannah's and see on the hilltop a little further up an outcrop of rocks looking very much like a miniature Stonehenge! Surely not! Panting to the top of this lonely road, and on inspection, it is indeed a circular ring of massive rocks standing up to the sky on this desolate rocky ridge looking out to sea. With no information panels, we're at a total loss on what they are but smile knowing that either Vincent or our neurotic landlady will no doubt hold the keys of knowledge.

Olly smiles and pats her belly. "I reckon we've worked up a bit of an appetite, and it would be foolish not to eat up all that delicious crab!"

Licking my lips, I nod in agreement, and we quickly march back down the hill, through the front door, and towards the kitchen. Politely knocking on the door, we hear her shout out for us to come in. Already seated at the kitchen table is a large, stern looking man, while Hannah is standing over a bowl with flour covered hands.

"Is it OK if we finish off the crab for lunch?"

"Of course. Bring it here and join us. I'm just making some Irish treacle brown bread, which we can all have later. Maria, my Spanish au pair, has gone out to get some vegetables for tonight's dinner, so you're more than welcome to join us for that too before we all sit down for the *Eurovision Song Contest*! Oh, and by the way, this is my neighbour, John Cuffe. If there's anyone who's got a story, it's got to be him!"

Olly and I sit down around the table with our massive bowl of crab claws, and before our hands get too mucky, we lean over and shake hands with John. The polite, conversation topics begin with the state of the weather, the general Irish economy, and who'll win tonight! Then, like you do, I ask, "So, John, what do you do?"

He coughs, "Well, I've done a lot of stuff in my life, like most folk, but for most of it I was a prison officer and at the time when there was a lot of violence here in Ireland."

We sit forward in curious anticipation, and he continues, "I entered Mountjoy in Dublin, nicknamed The Joy, as a young prison officer in 1978 and feel like I stepped back into Victorian times. I knew nothing about jails, apart from what I'd seen in black and white films on RTE; 'good' sheriffs and 'bad' hombres. I quickly learned that behind the bars, with The Joy holding the largest prison population in Ireland, there is no black and white and that the 'bad' guy often came in the guise of officialdom. So, there I saw the raw truth of thirty years working on the inside. I worked in Portlaoise, then Europe's top-security prison, and served in the drug-infested prisoners' Training Unit and witnessed the Spike Island riot—now that's Ireland's Alcatraz at the entrance to Cork Harbour! I remember waking up that day on the mainland in August 1985 and seeing Cork Harbour ablaze. A riot had broken out, and fires raged on the island all night. By dawn, most of the buildings on the island were aflame. The place was totally, totally unsuitable for prisoners. And over the years, I can count among my charges the IRA kidnappers of Dutchman Tiede Herrema, the gangsters implicated in Veronica Guerin's murder, and Dean Lyons, wrongly accused of the 1997 Grangegorman killings."

At this point, he rustles a thick tattered paperback, *Inside the Monkey House*, out of his bag and pushes it over the table. "Take a look while you're here. I wrote all about it in my book. We all did time, staff and prisoners alike. Each of us had a number, and we all wanted to finally get out of those gates. It's a pretty vivid and eye-opening story I tell of that archaic and chaotic prison system with all those secrets held behind those prison walls."

By now we're sitting to attention and respectfully stand up to shake his hand as he waves goodbye to us all and wanders out. By now, the oven has been turned on, and we see Hannah bashing a ball of dough to death on the top before squeezing it into an oblong loaf tin.

Hannah smiles, "Now girls onto something a little more light-hearted. You could make this Irish treacle bread at home; it's delicious. I'll show you how to make it. First of all, you need to mix all the dry ingredients together. So, you get eleven ounces of wholemeal flour, six ounces of white flour, three tablespoons of bran, two tablespoons of wheatgerm, a sprinkling of salt, two teaspoons of heaped baking powder, and mix it all up with your hands or a knife. Then add a dessert spoon of black treacle or molasses and just a bit of milk to create a sloppy wet dough. You can also add some seeds into the dough if you want. Make sure to generously butter the loaf tin really well, which will create a nice crispy crust. Then just plonk the dough in the tin like I'm doing now and cook for about twenty minutes in a hot oven, probably maximum 200 centigrade. You'll smell it soon and won't resist having a nice buttered slab! Also, you can make our Irish soda bread in the same way with bicarbonate of soda and buttermilk."

Olly claps her hands, "Fantastic! And what about that old stone circle we saw at the top of the road?"

Hannah giggles, "Oh no, it's not that old! There are a series of contemporary art structures that have recently been put up and on display as a sculpture trail across Ireland, and that's one of them, but I'm afraid I don't know any more!"

That evening, it feels like a large part of Europe is watching the *Eurovision Song Contest* from this remote living room, with Ireland, Wales, England, and Spain patriotically clapping away to the support their respective singers. Sods of peat are thrown into the crackling fireplace. A Guinness steak stew with ample servings of Mamee's homemade mash are served up, and then hearty apple crumble is eaten in front of the television while we all continue to politely tap our feet to the terrible music! Ironically, this is surely one of the loneliest, most remote places on our entire trip across Ireland but definitely one we'll remember with the most stories, warmest hospitality, and memories!

The next morning, ready to leave the wild Mullet Peninsula, the skies are miserably grey and ominous as our landlady waves us goodbye, together with an interesting surfing dude who'd turned up late the previous night from Dublin in search of wild waves known to exist in the area. The waterproofs are pulled on, as the weather forecasts have predicted that we're unfortunately going to encounter some rain today, which we've miraculously missed for the majority of our incredible two-week trip. We're finally leaving and saying goodbye to the glorious Atlantic and the wonderful roads we've ridden through. I remember an Irish biker called Stephen I'd met at one of the festivals saying, "Well (if you haven't visited) you've probably missed some of the best biking coastal roads you could find anywhere. Till you've been here you'll not understand the re-occurring call to return, despite the clouds." And that I'll toast to in total agreement!

We have a fairly large number of miles to get under our belts today, heading south-easterly inland into the counties of Roscommon and Longford, which form part of the fairly unknown pastoral landscapes of The Midlands area. So, without too much debate, we reach a happy consensus to take the more direct but busier N5. And without too much prompting, shortly after we've started out, the rain starts to pelt down in rods along the boring dual carriageways. Less than a few hours into the journey, I ride up alongside Olly and also see in her weather-beaten face that we need some respite from the rain and to find a warming, hot drink. The indicators are put on, and we ride through the fairly nondescript grey town of Foxford, famous for its woollen mills and their characteristic wool blankets, in search of some form of warmth and shelter. The rain has thankfully stopped by the time we park up, but there's still a cold, sharp wind. With no teashops in sight, we end up slumming it on a pavement bench in front of a supermarket with paper cups of coffee warming our hands and hot pasties warming our laps.

I notice Olly uncomfortably crossing her legs and in sympathy chirp up, "Don't worry, we'll ride down the road to the leisure centre we passed, where I'm sure we can sneak into and find some loos!"

Finally, at Longford we get off the main road and head south onto the beautiful R397 to the pretty rural town of Ballymahon. Further on we ride along a small green-leafed country road and through a set of impressive iron gates into beautiful parkland to find the idyllic Castlecor House, which was once a princely hunting lodge. This feels like the epitome of a glorious Irish Georgian abode that you'd easily see featured on the front of *Country Life* magazine, with its dogs barking and a smiling hostess coming to greet us from the grandeur of her home. We're led into sumptuous guest rooms, and after we've taken our wet clothes off and warmed ourselves with steamy hot showers, we sit next to a burning log fire in the stately but homely lounge.

But this isn't any old country house and is more than eccentric! It has, in fact, incredible architectural significance, as we're shown up the large stately stairs to a gigantic octagonal room, and rather like William Jones's Rotunda at Chelsea, there are four massive hearths set together, back to back, in the middle of this eighteenth century space with its highly coved ceiling. This place was designed for wear and comfort during the hunting season, but everything is over the top in magnificence, from Greek and Egyptian style decoration, decorative panels, to Corinthian columns—and all looking out through windows onto the green Irish countryside. But the place has seen better days, changing lives as a convent to an old people's home, and now simply needs a lot of TLC and refurbishment, which the owners, who've just bought it as a private family home, intend to do! That evening, we choose to pop into town for a tasty meal and roaring peat fire at Pat Skelly's in Ballymahon. Unsurprisingly, behind the bar is an incredible and massive selection of whiskeys sourced from distilleries all over Ireland. We stretch our feet out towards the warm fire while sipping our glasses of Guinness and laugh out loud again when we remember what our landlady back in Blacksod told us: "If you two girls landed in a bucket of shite, you'd still come up smelling o' roses." We'll toast to that! Although we end up returning to our country abode with a dodgy taxi driver, who swerves uncontrollably all over the place, having probably had one too many tipples, our evening's completed with further whiskey tastings from the generous collection laid out for us in the lounge.

And with that thought of whiskey, our Irish trip just wouldn't have been complete if we do not venture to find an authentic whiskey distillery somewhere along the way! And this new day, on a Monday morning, is the perfect time for such a recce. Coincidentally, our route back to the ferry port of Rosslare in the next couple of days was planned to go inland, through lesser known areas and, by pure chance, was passing through Kilbeggan. This is where the famous Kilbeggan Distillery is, established in 1757 and believed to be the world's oldest licensed distillery in the world, and still producing top quality whiskey!

Just a short skip and a hop down the R389, past the Kilbeggan racecourse—the only National Hunt course in Ireland—and we're parked up outside the white stone distillery in Kilbeggan. And after an hour's fascinating walk around hulking machinery, watching the mashing and fermenting, witnessing the mouthwatering beauty of oak casks full of whiskey, and not forgetting the obligatory connoisseur-tasting experience, we return to the bikes with a couple of bottles under each arm.

The sun's out and the day's looking good, so without further hesitation, I remind Olly of our conversation the previous night, "You know it's something I really wanted to do on this trip, and unbelievably, it's on our way. We won't even need to make any detours. Are you still alright for us to head to Kildare and visit the Irish National Stud?"

Olly smiles, "I know nothing about horses, but hey, another experience among the many we've already had here in Ireland, so why not?"

With the bottles of whiskey securely wrapped and protected around our clothes, we take off down the tiny country lanes of County Offaly, including a ride along a disused railway track in this beautiful lost countryside. Before too long, we've entered the endless rolling green pastures of thoroughbred country, County Kildare, home to many of Ireland's 300 stud farms. It has some of Ireland's best grazing farmland, making it a place for prime agricultural real estate.

Racing is the sport of kings and queens, plumbers and plasterers, and nowhere is the horse more at home than in Ireland. England may claim to be the home of flat racing, but what is not in doubt is that racing over jumps is entirely an Irish innovation. The first steeplechase—a cross-country horse race over obstacles—took place in County Cork in 1752. Two Irish gentlemen agreed to race from Buttevant Church to the Saint Leger Church across four and a half miles of open country, jumping any fence, wall, ditch, or hedge in their path. From this small beginning grew one of the most exciting sports, christened steeplechasing, after the tendency of early riders using church spires, visible far across the countryside, as finishing points. And nowhere is the place of the horse better symbolised than in the sumptuous surroundings of the Irish National Stud, close to the town of Kildare and west of Dublin. Some of the greatest horses in living memory have either been born or resided here as breeding stallions, including the legendary Arkle. Breeders from around the world send mares to be mated with the stallions and pay eye-watering sums, from the price of a car to the price of a house, depending on the stallion's popularity.

We park the bikes up and walk into the immaculate eight hundred acre site, which is also home to some incredible Japanese Gardens. The founder, Colonel William Hall Walker, in the early 1900s had a passion for racehorses but also astrology and believed that if any of his foals were born under the wrong star signs, he would sell them on! His love of horticulture also created these magnificent gardens, arguably the most beautiful in Europe. After a little walk into the Foaling Unit, where at this time of the year in May we're lucky enough to see adorable newly born, possible champions, we head to the stallions' block. Each stallion here is treated like a Hollywood star in their thick hay-lined stables. Each one has their own adjoining paddock, where the sound of loud and excited competitive whinnying is almost deafening. The money we're talking about is astronomical when we see the copper plates screwed on their stable doors: Decorated Knight—1,512,000 million euros prize money, Invincible Spirit—with his fee of 120,000 euros, his yearlings go on to sell in the region of 900,000 euros! These animals are literally priceless.

And then with a pounding heart, I notice the main reason for the visit. A symbolic brass plate shines next to one of the stables—Sea The Stars (Cape Cross—Urban Sea)—Multiple Group 1 Winning Champion was foaled here at the Irish National Stud 6th April 2006 at 23:20 weighing 66 kg / 142 lbs. It's in this one moment that I reflect back to 2009 and that incredible year that he and I both literally went on a ride of discovery, risk, thrills, and winnings! I touch the plaque, grateful and happy I'd somehow known him. He's kept now just a few miles down the road at the Aga Khan's Gilltown stud in Kilcullen, whose high security gates and walls we curiously pass when we're back on the road heading southwards. With just a few days left before leaving this amazing place called Ireland, this last visit seems to have naturally made the trip come full circle in creating even stronger ties with the country.

The peaceful, narrow lanes on this late sunny afternoon lead us just a few miles further into the little-visited and hidden place of County Laois (pronounced leash) and the village of Stradbally, where groceries are picked up from SuperValu for an outdoor feast later on. Further up the road, we enter a concealed driveway and are met by another old, ivy and wisteria clad country house. No one is here, just a welcoming message and instructions on where the rooms can be found, which we find are nestled in the attic space. The cobwebbed windows create a little bit of theatrical presence, but unfortunately, the new bath has no taps or running water! The picnic is laid out on the grass under an old oak tree, and for a few moments, I just lie down silently, closing my eyes and absorbing the positive surroundings and pure tranquillity of this beautiful place.

I hear a cough, open my eyes, and see Olly's kindly brought out a large salad, fresh bread, fruit, and a bottle of local apple juice piled onto a big tray.

Plates are handed out, and Olly murmurs, "It feels like, not for the first time, we've got this whole place to ourselves. I wonder if we'll even see the hosts! I can't believe that this trip has almost come to an end. Just one more day getting to Rosslare and then the boat back."

I nod and sigh, "What a trip! We've had the most incredible, eclectic time possible, and you've been the perfect travelling companion. Thank you!"

Olly smiles in appreciation and raises her glass to toast our exploits, "But seriously, Zoë, are you telling the truth when you told me that you haven't really travelled on your motorbike with other people? We've had a scream!"

I sway my head from side to side in reflection, "Well not totally, and most of the time I do prefer my own company, but obviously you're the exception to that rule! But, you're right, nothing as long or as enjoyable as these past two weeks. I guess there have only been two other trips of any significance. The first was having just passed my test, and I met a nice enough girl at Merton Motorcycling College, near Wimbledon, where we were both doing a summer's bike mechanics course and getting used to our new two-wheel purchases. She had an old Yamaha, and at fairly short notice, we decided to hop over to Normandy for a few days. The only thing I really remember out of that trip was arriving in Le Havre, to then ride up and over the frighteningly gigantic and high Normandy Bridge to Honfleur. It was a pleasant enough trip, but the dynamics weren't really there."

Then I smile with a little twinkle in my eye, "And then a few years ago, again on the Triumph, I was invited to go to the TT Races on the Isle of Man."

Olly giggles, "Yes, I remember something about that. What happened exactly?"

"I'm sure I told you, but it was Mr, Sexy who invited me. He'd been a TT racer and knew the Isle of Man and all its roads inside out like the back of his hand. The offer was too good to refuse. We met up at a petrol station near Liverpool, and from that moment on, with me frantically racing behind him just to keep up, I knew the next few days would be a challenge, to say the least! The Isle of Man is beautiful, but with all the hundreds of other crazy riders out on the roads, after the first day I parked my bike up and was more than happy to accept the offer to ride as pillion. And what a blast that was! Racing up along the Mountain Mile from The Verandah, then stopping at Joey Dunlop's statue at Bungalow Bend, and sitting behind him was a one in a million. Over the next few days, we actually rode the entire thirty-seven mile mountain course at some pretty neck-breaking speeds. At times we were leaning so low around the corners that I felt my jacket brushing the ground and simply just closed my eyes and prayed to God that a tomorrow still existed. I was literally putting my life into somebody else's hands!"

The sun is slowly setting behind the old house, and before we know it, we'll be back out on the roads early the next morning. And indeed, the sun obligingly rises brightly for us in the morning, and looking over to the other bed, I see the sleepy face and ruffled hair of a Ken Dodd lookalike. Uncontrollable laughs break out from us both! Under a cloudless sky, having combed our hair down, we ride down to Stradbally Fayre Café to dig into plates of posh eggs Benedict. I tap my feet, bizarrely listening to Canned Heat belting out *On The Road Again*! and looking down at the now more than well-used maps, we agree on the final route back to Rosslare; the N80 all the way through County Wexford to finally join the N25.

For one last time, we start the bikes up for our last day out on the roads together, stopping along the way at the Irish National Heritage Park near Wexford then are welcomed to Rosslare by bright blues skies and the exotic tropical gardens of our hosts' house overlooking the Irish Sea and Rosslare Bay.

It's an early start the next day, but we have the luxury of a relaxed departure, with just a ten minute ride to the ferry. The boat is already there, and we're soon riding into it and strapping our bikes down. We quietly walk up the stairs with everybody else and now with the difficult prospect of finding comfortable, quiet seats for the whole journey.

But Olly turns to me and wickedly smiles, "I have a surprise for you! I've bought us an upgrade to a cabin with two beds, which means we can sleep and relax before our long rides back. We even have our own toilet and shower! It should make the ferry a lot more doable, and you could say the cherry on the cake in making this the perfect trip!"

Two weary but very happy girls take off their biking gear and flop onto the cosy bunk beds. The horns blast out, and very soon, the ship is leaving beautiful Ireland and taking us back home over that mystical stretch of water.

EPILOGUE

My final, mini-escapade planned to be included in this book was to be a short motorcycle trip in April 2020 with my good friend, Olly, to the delightful rugged island of Anglesey. But due to the world's pandemic, with the country in total shut-down, this had to be cancelled.

The world will never be quite the same again, and the perception of adventure travel will no doubt change. Wherever your travels take you in the future, may they be safe, happy, and fulfilling.

Carpe Diem—Live for the Day.

London, 2020

Appendix

Road and Sea Routes around the British Isles

ENGLAND TO FRANCE
The Solar Eclipse Sailing Route (August 1999)

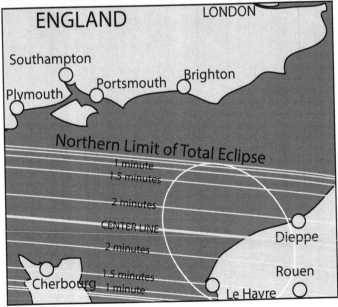

WALES

On the B roads by Scooter
From London to Borth via the English/Welsh Borderlands and the Elan Valley
Total 346 miles (September 2017)

Day 1—Walton-on-Thames to Hereford—131 miles
Day 2—Hereford to Saint Harmon, Rhayader (and through the Elan Valley)—53 miles
Day 3—Saint Harmon to Corris—34 miles
Day 4—Corris and Southern Snowdonia
Day 5—Corris to Borth—42 miles
Day 6—Borth to Cwmerfyn via Aberystwyth—14 miles
Day 7—Cwmerfyn to Hereford—77 miles

"Chasing the Welsh Red Dragon"
Circular Coastal Motorcycle Ride around Wales
Total 543 miles (July 2016)

Hereford to Llangollen—109 miles
Llangollen to Abersoch via Llanberis Pass, Snowdonia—99 miles
Abersoch to Barmouth—54 miles
Barmouth to Aberaeron—79 miles
Aberaeron to Mwnt Beach—23 miles
Mwnt Beach to Aberdare in The Valleys—130 miles
Aberdare to Hereford via the Brecon Beacons and Black Mountains—49 miles

With John McGuinness at Aberdare Road Races, Wales

SCOTLAND
The Highlands, North Coast "NC500," & Isle of Skye
with Snatches of Northumberland & the Lake District
Total 1,962 miles (September 2019)

Day 1—London to Bamburgh, Northumberland via Alnwick—288 miles

Day 2—Bamburgh across into Scotland to Loch Lomond via "The Kelpies"—164 miles

Day 3—Loch Lomond to Camusdarach—135 miles

Day 4—Camusdarach to Mallaig return and back—10 miles

Day 5—Camusdarach to Fortrose Bay and Chanonry Point on The Black Isle—139 miles

Day 6—The Black Isle to Dunnet Bay via John O' Groats, Wick—147 miles

Day 7—Dunnet Bay to Achmelvich—145 miles

Day 8—Achmelvich to Applecross—155 miles

Day 9—Applecross to Glen Brittle, Isle of Skye via the ferry—100 miles

Day 10—Isle of Skye to Loch Lomond—278 miles

Day 11—Loch Lomond to Thornthwaite, Keswick in the Lake District, England —167 miles

Day 12—Keswick to Hereford—234 miles

John o' Groats, Scotland

IRELAND
Our Wild Atlantic Way & Connemara
Total within Ireland 785 miles (May 2019)

Day 1—Hereford to Goodwick, Wales—134 miles; Ferry from Goodwick, Wales to Rosslare, Ireland—48 miles; Rosslare to Mullinavat—42 miles

Day 2—Mullinavat to Galway—163 miles

Day 3—Galway—4 walking miles in and out of pubs!

Day 4—Galway to Roundstone—100 miles

Day 5—Roundstone to Leenane and Killary Harbour—47.5 miles

Day 6—Leenane day trips—19 miles

Day 7—Leenane day trips—28.5 miles

Day 8—Leenane to Achill Island—84 miles

Day 9—Achill Island to Blacksod Bay, Mullet Peninsula— 75 miles

Day 10—Blacksod Bay area—3 walking miles

Day 11—Blacksod Bay, Mullet Peninsula to Castlecor—140 miles

Day 12—Castlecor to Stradbally—82 miles

Day 13—Stradbally to Rosslare—75 miles

Day 14—Rosslare, Ireland to Hereford, England—182 miles

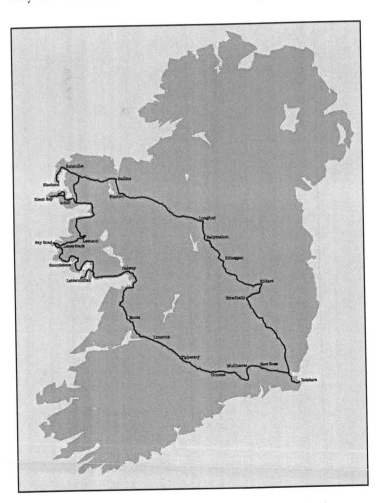

REFERNCE AND READING

*With a Pinch of Salt—A Collection of Nautical Expressions &
Other Stories* by Captain Nick Bates

Independent Hostel Guide: England, Wales & Scotland www.
independenthostels.co.uk

Scotland's Highlands and Islands, Lonely Planet

*Ireland's Blue Book—Irish Country Houses, Historic Hotels
and Restaurants*

Ireland; Land, People, History by Richard Killeen

Lonely Planet's *Best of Ireland—Top Sights, Authentic
Experiences*

Ireland's Best Trips, Lonely Planet

Irish Tourist Advisory Service—*Souvenir Guide & Map West
& Best 500 Mile Scenic Tour*

Out on a Limb by Shirley MacLaine

Jonathan Livingston Seagull by Richard Bach

Campervan Conversions—Newlands Vans, rodfinlayson80@
gmail.com

Also by Zoë Cano
Bonneville Go or Bust

In life we all have dreams. But do we ever attempt to make them happen?

A true story with a difference. She had nothing. No money. No time. No motorbike. No experience for such a mammoth trip. But she did have a clear vision. So with gritted determination, she goes all out to make her dream come true: to travel solo and unassisted across the lesser-known roads of the North American continent covering more than 8,000 km on a classic Triumph Bonneville.

From the outset to the end of this escapade, it's always going to be a question of "Go or Bust" on whether she'll ever succeed or even finish the journey with the most unexpected obstacles, dangers and surprises that come her way. Her wry sense of humour helps without doubt, get her out of some of anyone's worst case scenarios.

An inspiring and motivational story written with passion to succeed against all odds, a true life lesson in believing in yourself—there is no such thing as dreaming too big.

So let the adventure begin!

Also from Road Dog Publications

Bonneville Go or Bust[1][2] by Zoë Cano
A true story with a difference. Zoë had no experience for such a mammoth adventure of a lifetime but goes all out to make her dream come true to travel solo across the lesser known roads of the American continent on a classic motorcycle.

I loved reading this book. She has a way of putting you right into the scene. It was like riding on the back seat and experiencing this adventure along with Zoë.—★★★★ Amazon Review

Southern Escapades[1][2] by Zoë Cano
As an encore to her cross country trip, Zoë rides along the tropical Gulf of Mexico and Atlantic Coast in Florida, through the forgotten back roads of Alabama and Georgia. This adventure uncovers the many hidden gems of lesser known places in these beautiful Southern states.

. . . Zoë has once again interested and entertained me with her American adventures. Her insightful prose is a delight to read and makes me want to visit the same places.—★★★★★ Amazon Review

Chilli, Skulls & Tequila[1][2] by Zoë Cano
Zoe captures the spirit of beautiful Baja California, Mexico, with a solo 3 000 mile adventure encountering a myriad of surprises along the way and unique, out-of-the-way places tucked into Baja's forgotten corners.

Zoe adds hot chilli and spices to her stories, creating a truly mouth-watering reader's feast!—★★★★ Amazon Review

Hellbent for Paradise[1][2] by Zoë Cano
The inspiring—and often nail-biting—tale of Zoë's exploits roaming the jaw-dropping natural wonders of New Zealand on a mission to find her own paradise.

Motorcycles, Life, and . . . [1][2] by Brent Allen

Sit down at a table and talk motorcycles, life and . . . (fill in the blank) with award winning riding instructor and creator of the popular "Howzit Done?" video series, Brent "Capt. Crash" Allen. Here are his thoughts about riding and life and how they combine told in a lighthearted tone.

The Elemental Motorcyclist [1][2] by Brent Allen

Brent's second book offers more insights into life and riding and how they go together. This volume, while still told in the author's typical easy-going tone, gets down to more specifics about being a better rider.

A Short Ride in the Jungle [1][2] by Antonia Bolingbroke-Kent

A young woman tackles the famed Ho Chi Minh Trail alone on a diminutive pink Honda Cub armed only with her love of Southeast Asia, its people, and her wits.

Beads in the Headlight [1] by Isabel Dyson

A British couple tackle riding from Alaska to Tierra del Fuego two-up on a 31 year-old BMW "airhead." Join them on this epic journey across two continents.

A great blend of travel, motorcycling, determination, and humor. — ★★★★★
Amazon Review

Chasing America [1][2] by Tracy Farr

Tracy Farr sets off on multiple legs of a motorcycle ride to the four corners of America in search of the essence of the land and its people.

In Search of Greener Grass [1] by Graham Field

With game show winnings and his KLR 650, Graham sets out solo for Mongolia & beyond. Foreword by Ted Simon

Eureka [1] by Graham Field

Graham sets out on a journey to Kazahkstan only to realize his contrived goal is not making him happy. He has a "Eureka!" moment, turns around, and begins to enjoy the ride as the ride itself becomes the destination.

Different Natures[1] *by Graham Field*
The story of two early journeys Graham made while living in the US, one north to Alaska and the other south through Mexico. Follow along as Graham tells the stories in his own unique way.

Thoughts on the Road[1][2] *by Michael Fitterling*
The Editor of *Vintage Japanese Motorcycle Magazine* ponders his experiences with motorcycles and riding and how they've intersected and influenced his life.

Northeast by Northwest[1][2] *by Michael Fitterling*
The author finds two motorcycle journeys of immense help staving off depression and the other effects of stress. Along the way, he discovers the beauty of North America and the kindness of its people.

. . . one of the most captivating stories I have read in a long time. Truly a MUST read!!—★★★★★ Amazon Review

Hit the Road, Jac![1][2] *by Jacqui Furneaux*
At 50, Jacqui leaves her home and family, buys a motorcycle in India, and begins a seven-year world-wide journey with no particular plan. Along the way she comes to terms with herself and her family.

Asphalt & Dirt[1][2] *by Aaron Heinrich*
A compilation of profiles of both famous figures in the motorcycle industry and relatively unknown people who ride, dispelling the myth of the stereotypical "biker" image.

A Tale of Two Dusters & Other Stories[1][2] *by Kirk Swanick*
In this collection of tales, Kirk Swanick tells of growing up a gearhead behind both the wheels of muscle cars and the handlebars of motorcycles and describes the joys and trials of riding

Man in the Saddle[1][2] *by Paul van Hoof*
Aboard a 1975 Moto Guzzi V7, Paul starts out from Alaska for Ushuaia. Along the way there are many twists and turns, some which change his life forever. English translation from the original Dutch.

Shiny Side Up[1][2] by Ron Davis
A delightful collection of essays and articles from Ron Davis, Associate Editor and columnist for *BMW Owners News*. This book is filled with tales of the road and recounts the joys and foibles of motorcycle ownership and maintenance. Read it and find out why Ron is a favorite of readers of the *Owners News*!

Those Two Idiots![1][2] by A. P. Atkinson
Mayhem, mirth, and adventure follow two riders across two continents. Setting off for Thailand thinking they were prepared, this story if full of mishaps and triumphs. An honest journey with all the highs and lows, wins and losses, wonderful people and low-lifes, and charms and pitfalls of the countries traveled through.

Morocco Road[1][2] by Ragnar Hojland Espinosa
The author has big dreams of a round-the-world ride, but reality makes him rethink the huge scope of that endeavor, and he truncates his dream for the time being, but instead "gets his feet wet" on the dusty roads of Morocco trying this thing they call "adventure travel."

Don't Tell Mama I'm Going to Mongolia on a Motorcycle[1][2] by Ricardo Fité
Every year, hundreds of people raise money for charity by participating in the Mongol Rally, a dangerous un-routed expedition that only has a starting and finishing point. In 2011 Spanish motorbiker, Ricardo Fité, participated in this dangerous adventure on his classic 1990s' dual sport motorbike, traveling through all of Eastern Europe, Russia, and into the heart of Central Asia, all while facing difficulties, and challenges along the way.